WHAT'S COOKING

Mexican

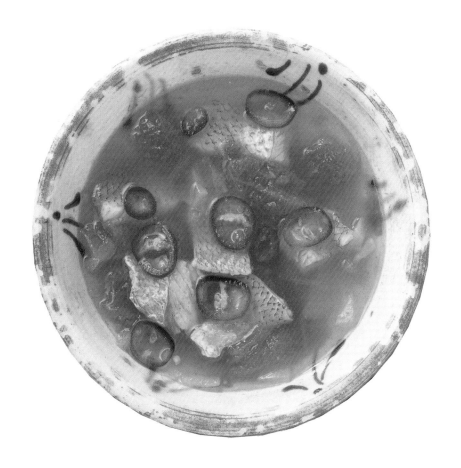

Marlena Spieler

THUNDER BAY
P·R·E·S·S

First published in the United States in 2000 by
Thunder Bay Press
An imprint of the Advantage Publishers Group
5880 Oberlin Drive
San Diego, CA 92121
www.advantagebooksonline.com

A Parragon book, Parragon, Queen Street House, 4 Queen Street, Bath BA1 1HE, UK

ISBN: 1-57145-253-2
Library of Congress Cataloging-in-Publication Data available upon requst.

Printed in Singapore

Acknowledgments

Editorial Consultant: Felicity Jackson
Photography: Colin Bowling, Paul Forrester and Stephen Brayne
Home Economist and Stylist: Vicki Smallwood

All props supplied by Barbara Stewart at Surfaces.

North American Edition
Managing Editor: JoAnn Padgett
Project Editor: Elizabeth McNulty

Note
Unless otherwise stated,
milk is assumed to be full fat, eggs are medium
and pepper is freshly ground black pepper.

Recipes using uncooked eggs should be avoided by infants,
the elderly, pregnant women, and anyone suffering from an illness.

Contents

Introduction

The cuisine of Mexico is a diverse and extraordinary cuisine, a complex layering of cultures, starting with the ancient Indian civilizations and built upon by the Spanish conquest as well as other European influences.

The soul of Mexican food lies in its ancient roots: Aztec, Toltec, Zapotec, Ohnec, and Mayan. Deeply colored, complex, rich sauces made of mild and hot chilies, seeds, herbs, and vegetables are as ancient as the cultures from which they come. Long stewed meats, such as the Spanish contribution of pork, figure prominently in the Mexican kitchen; the broth that comes about through the cooking makes soups that fuel everyday life and add flavor and depth to dishes of beans, rice, and stews. Fish from the coastlines that cover thousands of miles and define the shape of the country, are eaten cloaked with spicy pastes, splashed with chilies, wrapped in tortillas or fragrant leaves.

Over this ancient cuisine of indigenous foods and techniques lies a veneer of Spanish propriety and European tradition, as well as the imports from Spain: wheat (for those flour tortillas and the crusty bread rolls, *bolillos*), domesticated animals whose milk added cheese to the menu, and the pig! With its abundant fat, frying became possible, adding a new dimension to the cooking methods.

TORTILLAS

The tortilla—a thin pancake-like flat bread—is eaten for nearly every meal throughout Mexico. Eaten in the same way as bread to accompany dishes, they are also wrapped around food as an eating utensil.

In the north, wheat or flour tortillas will be the ones you will find most often; in the south they will be corn, sometimes blue corn. Tortillas may be tiny or huge, eaten fresh off the griddle (*comal*) or filled and fried; they form the basis of the foods of Mexico.

Wrapped around any filling, a corn tortilla becomes a *taco*, a flour tortilla a *burrito*. Fresh and warm, a corn tortilla is a soft taco, fried to a crisp it is a crisp taco. A flat crisply fried tortilla is a *tostada*—top them with a layer of warm refried beans, cheese, pickled chilies or salsa, salad, morsels of meat or vegetables.

Stale corn tortillas are never thrown away in the frugal Mexican kitchen, and the cuisine is all the better for it: dipped into spicy sauces then rolled around various fillings they make the wonderful casserole that is called *enchiladas*, or fried and layered with sauce they are called *chilaquiles*.

Most of us are familiar with tortilla chips—at their best when freshly made from stale corn tortillas, but also widely available ready-made.

BEANS

Beans, too, are basic, along with rice and chilies. In every marketplace cafe (*fonda*) and home kitchen, you'll find pots and *cazuelas* of beans simmering to tender, ready to be eaten in all of their guises, or just from a bowl with a few tortillas to roll around them to satisfy hunger.

Throughout Mexico, the types of beans vary delightfully, from the tender pale pink beans of the north, such as pinto, to the inky black beans of the south. Beans that are puréed and cooked in fat and spices are called refried beans, though they are not really fried at all, merely cooked down to an intense paste in a puddle of (traditional) lard or (contemporary) vegetable oil.

CHILLIES

Next to tortillas and beans, it is chilies that define Mexican food. They offer flavor, textures, colors, and aromas as well heat, and keep the often monotonous diet lively. They are eaten raw and cooked, sliced and stewed, stuffed and puréed, soaked and fried, and are eaten at every meal, usually in the form of a salsa to spoon on as desired. They are rich in antioxidant vitamins and will clear your sinuses pronto, not to mention their alleged aphrodisiac qualities.

Understandably, chilies can intimidate—they can be searingly hot and should be added a little at a time.

Mild chilies are usually eaten red and dried, though Mexicans also dote on crushed hot red chilies—usually a dried cayenne. Mild chilies such as *pasilla*, *ancho*, *mulatto,* and *negro* make up the distinctive flavorful mixture sold simply on our spice shelf as "mild chili powder."

Most fresh chilies are hot and hotter. *Jalapeño* are probably most often eaten, a good all-purpose little chili with a nice fiery heat and delicious flavor. *Serrano* is another popular fresh chili. In the Caribbean region *habanero* and Scotch bonnet peppers add their distinctive fire.

Two milder chilies, the Anaheim and *poblano* are utterly delicious eaten stuffed, as you would a pepper; if unavailable, use ordinary green peppers, roasted and marinated with a chopped fresh hot chili or two to enliven them.

Bottled hot seasonings are ubiquitous, too; you'll find one on practically every table as well as kitchen shelf: a nice jolt of tangy fire for those who dare.

OTHER FLAVORINGS

Mexican spicing, however, is not limited to chilies: cinnamon, cloves, black pepper, cocoa powder, and especially cumin are used with enthusiasm, as are the herbs of oregano, marjoram, mint, *epazote,* and fresh cilantro. Roasted onion and whole garlic cloves are often crushed to form the basis of a sauce, and wedges of lime or lemon are served with soups, meats, fish, almost everything, Mediterranean–style.

MEXICAN STYLE

Meals in Mexico are a never ending fiesta. The main meal, the *comida corrida*, is served Spanish style, in the afternoon. Breakfast may either be a light one of hot chocolate or coffee with sweet rolls or churros to dip in, or a hearty late breakfast *almuerzo*, often consisting of the exquisite egg dishes for which Mexico is so well known. The markets and their *fondas*, *cantinas*, and *taquerias*, beckon with their irresistible aromas, convincing you that you are indeed hungry, and an endless parade of *tacos, tostadas, enchiladas, burritos*, soups, shellfish, and grilled fish tantalize the palate.

And if your appetite is jaded from the sultry heat and feasting, and you don't have room for even one more *burrito*, persuade yourself to nibble a reviving snack—fresh fruit, such as pineapple, oranges, jicama, and mango—sprinkled with hot red pepper and served with a squeeze of lime juice. After that you will be ready for anything.

Soups & Starters

Start a Mexican meal in authentic style with vegetable soups highlighted with chili, citrus fruit, and garlic, or offer a delicate Mexican Fish & Roasted Tomato Soup to really get the taste buds tingling. Find out how Mexican cooks simmer meat to make a tasty stock that forms the basis of many of their delicious soups.

Mexico is famous for its Guacamole—a luscious avocado dip, lightly spiced and served with crunchy tortilla chips.—ideal as a light starter or as a dip with drinks. For light bites to get a meal off to a good start, you can't beat little wedges of tortilla topped with chorizo, artichoke hearts, and cheese, or everyone's favorite, Nachos—a luscious combination of tortilla chips, refried beans, and melted cheese, topped with avocado and salad.

Refreshing seafood cocktails and marinated fish are specialities of the Mexican cuisine and provide a cooling opener to a meal, while Spicy-sweet Meat Empanadas are delicious appetizers, perfect for parties. Whether you choose to serve tiny rolls of tortilla, filling with tantalizing Mexican ingredients, or a salad of crunchy raw vegetables, spiced with chili, you'll find something here to interest and entice.

Mexican Citrus Soup

Roasted onion and garlic are combined with tangy citrus flavors to create a soup full of tantalizing tastes.

Serves 4

INGREDIENTS

2 onions
15 large garlic cloves, unpeeled
1 tbsp. extra-virgin olive oil
6 cups vegetable, chicken or fish stock
1 cup water
8 ripe tomatoes, diced
pinch of dried oregano
1 fresh green chili, such as jalapeño or

serrano, deseeded and chopped
pinch of ground cumin
½ tsp. finely grated grapefruit rind
½ tsp. finely grated lime rind
½ tsp. finely grated orange rind
juice and diced flesh of 2 limes
juice of 1 orange
juice of 1 grapefruit

salt and pepper

TO GARNISH:
tortilla chips, or sliced tortilla strips
  fried until crisp
2 tbsp. chopped fresh cilantro

1 Cut one onion in half without peeling. Peel and finely chop the second onion.

2 Heat a large heavy-based frying pan, add the unpeeled onion halves and garlic and cook over a medium-high heat until the skins char and the onions are caramelized on their cut sides; the garlic should be soft on the inside. Remove the onion and garlic from the pan and set aside until cool enough to handle.

3 Meanwhile, heat the oil in a pan and lightly sauté the remaining onion until softened. Add the stock and water and bring to a boil. Reduce the heat and simmer for a few minutes.

4 Peel the charred onion and garlic, then chop coarsely and add to the simmering soup, together with the tomatoes, chili, oregano, and cumin. Cook for about 15 minutes, stirring occasionally.

5 Add the citrus rind, season with salt and pepper, then simmer for a further 2 minutes. Remove from the heat and stir in the lime flesh and citrus juices.

6 Ladle into soup bowls, garnish with tortilla chips and fresh cilantro, and serve immediately.

Spicy Gazpacho

This classic Spanish cold soup is given a Mexican twist by adding chilies and fresh cilantro. Serve with chunks of bread to for a refreshing start to a meal.

Serves 4-6

INGREDIENTS

1 cucumber
2 green bell peppers
½ fresh hot chili
6 ripe flavorful tomatoes
½-1 onion, finely chopped
3-4 garlic cloves, chopped
4 tbsp. extra-virgin olive oil

¼-½ tsp. ground cumin
2 tsp. sherry vinegar, or a
 combination of balsamic vinegar
 and wine vinegar
4 tbsp. chopped fresh cilantro
2 tbsp. chopped fresh parsley
1½ cups tomato juice or canned

chopped tomatoes
salt and pepper
ice cubes, to serve

1 Peel the cucumber, cut it in half lengthways, then cut into quarters. Remove the seeds with a teaspoon, then dice the flesh. Cut the peppers in half, remove the cores and seeds, then dice the flesh. Deseed and chop the chili.

2 If you prefer to skin the tomatoes, place in a heatproof bowl, pour boiling water over to cover and stand for 30 seconds. Drain and plunge into cold water. The skins will then slide off easily.

Cut the tomatoes in half, deseed if wished, then chop the flesh.

3 Combine half the cucumber, green bell pepper, tomatoes and onion in a blender or food processor with all the chili, garlic, olive oil, cumin, vinegar, cilantro, and parsley. Process with enough of the tomato juice to make a smooth purée.

4 Pour the puréed soup into a bowl and stir in the remaining green bell pepper, cucumber, tomatoes and onion. Season with salt and pepper to taste, then cover and chill for a few hours.

5 To serve, stir, ladle into soup bowls and add 1–2 ice cubes to each portion.

COOK'S TIP

Freeze tomato juice ice-cubes as a delicious alternative.

Spicy Zucchini Soup with Rice & Lime

Mild red chili powder and pan-browned garlic give flavor to this simple, comforting soup. Quick to make, it's ideal for a light lunch.

Serves 4

INGREDIENTS

2 tbsp. oil
4 garlic cloves, thinly sliced
1-2 tbsp. mild red chili powder
¼-½ tsp. ground cumin

6¼ cups chicken, vegetable or beef stock
2 zucchini, cut into bite-sized chunks
6 tbsp. long-grain rice

salt and pepper
fresh oregano sprigs, to garnish
lime wedges, to serve (optional)

1 Heat the oil in a heavy-based pan, add the garlic and fry for about 2 minutes until softened and just beginning to change color. Add the chili powder and cumin and cook over a medium-low heat for a minute.

2 Stir in the stock, zucchini, and rice, then cook over medium-high heat for about 10 minutes until the zucchini are just tender and the rice is cooked through. Season the soup with salt and pepper.

3 Ladle into soup bowls, garnish with oregano and serve with lime wedges.

COOK'S TIP

Instead of rice, use rice-shaped pasta, such as orzo, or very thin pastas known as fideo. Use yellow summer squash instead of the zucchini and add cooked pinto beans in place of, or together with, the rice. Diced tomatoes also make a tasty addition.

VARIATIONS

Choose zucchini which are firm to the touch and have shiny skin. They should not be too large.

Mexican Vegetable Soup with Tortilla Chips

Crisp tortilla chips act as croûtons in this hearty vegetable soup which is found throughout Mexico. Add cheese to melt in, if you wish, and make the soup as hot tasting as you like!

Serves 4-6

INGREDIENTS

2 tbsp. vegetable or extra-virgin olive oil
1 onion, finely chopped
4 garlic cloves, finely chopped
¼–½ tsp. ground cumin
2-3 tsp. mild chili powder, such as ancho or New Mexico
1 carrot, sliced
1 waxy potato, diced
1½ cups diced fresh or canned tomatoes

1 zucchini, diced
¼ small cabbage, diced
4 cups vegetable or chicken stock or water
1 ear of corn, the kernels cut off of the cob, or 3 oz. canned corn
about 10 green beans, topped and tailed, then cut into bite-sized lengths
salt and pepper

TO SERVE:
4-6 tbsp. chopped fresh cilantro
salsa of your choice, or chopped fresh chili, to taste

1 Heat the oil in a heavy-based pan. Add the onion and garlic and cook for a few minutes until softened, then sprinkle in the cumin and chili. Stir in the carrot, potato, tomatoes, zucchini, and cabbage and cook for 2 minutes, stirring occasionally.

2 Pour in the stock. Cover and cook over a medium heat for about 20 minutes until the vegetables are tender.

3 Add extra water if necessary, then stir in the corn and green beans and cook for a further 5-10 minutes or until the beans are

tender. Season with salt and pepper to taste, bearing in mind that the tortilla chips may be salty.

4 Ladle the soup into soup bowls and sprinkle each portion with fresh cilantro. Top with salsa or chili, then add tortilla chips and a wedge of lime. Serve at once.

Crab & Cabbage Soup

From the Vera Cruz region, this delicious soup uses fresh crab meat to add a rich flavor to a mildly spicy vegetable and fish broth.

Serves 4

INGREDIENTS

1 whole cooked crab or 6-8 oz. crab meat
¼ cabbage
1 lb. ripe tomatoes
4 cups stock or water mixed with 1-2 fish (or chicken) stock cubes
1 onion, thinly sliced

1 small carrot, diced
4 garlic cloves, finely chopped
6 tbsp. chopped fresh cilantro
1 tsp. mild chili powder, such as New Mexico
pinch of dried oregano leaves, crumbled
salt and pepper

TO SERVE:
1-2 limes, cut into wedges
salsa of your choice

1 Cut out any thick stalk from the cabbage, then shred finely using a large knife.

2 To skin the tomatoes, place in a heatproof bowl, pour boiling water over to cover and stand for 30 seconds. Drain and plunge into cold water. The skins will then slide off easily. Chop the skinned tomatoes.

3 Place the tomatoes and stock in a pan with the onion, carrot, cabbage, garlic, fresh cilantro, and chili powder. Bring to a boil, then reduce the heat and simmer for about 20 minutes until the vegetables are just tender.

4 Remove the crab meat from the whole crab, if using. Twist off the legs and claws and crack with a rolling pin. Remove the flesh from the legs with a skewer. Remove the body section from the main crab shell and remove the meat, discarding the stomach bag and feathery gills.

5 Add the oregano and crab meat to the pan and simmer for 10-15 minutes to combine the flavors. Season with salt and pepper.

6 Ladle into soup bowls and serve with a wedge of lime. Pass around the salsa separately.

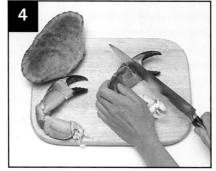

Mexican Fish
& Roasted Tomato Soup

Mexico's long shoreline yields an abundance of fish and shellfish, which are often turned into spicy, satisfying soups.

Serves 4

INGREDIENTS

5 ripe tomatoes

5 garlic cloves, unpeeled

1 lb. 2 oz. snapper, cut into chunks

4 cups fish stock, or water plus a fish

stock cube or two

2–3 tbsp. olive oil

1 onion, chopped

2 fresh green chilies, such as serrano,

deseeded and thinly sliced

lime wedges, to serve

1 Heat an ungreased heavy-based frying pan, add the whole tomatoes and garlic and char over a high heat or under a preheated broiler. The skins of the vegetables should blacken and char, and the flesh inside should be tender. Alternatively, place the tomatoes and garlic cloves in a roasting pan and bake in a preheated oven at 375–400° F for about 40 minutes.

2 Leave the tomatoes and garlic to cool, then remove the skins and chop coarsely, combining them with any juices from the pan. Set aside.

3 Poach the snapper in the stock over medium just until it is opaque and firmish. Remove from the heat and set aside.

4 Heat the oil in a pan and cook the chopped onion until softened. Strain in the cooking liquid from the fish, then add the chopped tomatoes and garlic. Bring to a boil, then reduce the heat and simmer for about 5 minutes to combine the flavors. Add the serrano chilies.

5 Divide chunks of the poached fish between soup bowls, ladle over the soup and serve with lime wedges for squeezing over.

Chicken, Avocado, & Chipotle Soup

This soup evolved from the foodstalls that line the streets of Tlalpan, a suburb of Mexico City: rich avocado, shreds of chicken, and the smoky hit of chipotle make it special.

Serves 4

INGREDIENTS

6 ¼ cups chicken stock

2-3 garlic cloves, finely chopped

1-2 chipotle chilies, cut into very thin strips (see Cook's Tip)

1 avocado

lime or lemon juice, for tossing

3-5 scallions, thinly sliced

12–14 oz. cooked chicken breast meat, torn or cut into shreds or thin strips

2 tbsp. chopped fresh cilantro

TO SERVE:

1 lime, cut into wedges

handful of tortilla chips (optional)

1 Place the stock in a pan with the garlic and chipotle chilies and bring to a boil.

2 Meanwhile, cut the avocado in half around the pit. Twist apart, then remove the pit with a knife. Carefully peel off the skin, dice the flesh, and toss in lime or lemon juice to prevent discoloration.

3 Arrange the scallions, chicken, avocado, and fresh cilantro in the base of 4 soup bowls or in a large serving bowl.

4 Ladle the hot stock over, and serve each bowl with lime and a handful of tortilla chips if using.

VARIATION

Add a drained 14 oz can garbanzo beans to the bowls in Step 3.

COOK'S TIP

Chipotle chilies are smoked and dried jalapeño chilies and are available canned or dried from specialty stores. They add a distinctive smoky flavor to dishes and are very hot. Use chipotles canned in adobo marinade for this recipe, if possible. Drain the canned version before using. Dried chipotles need to be reconstituted before using (see page 100).

Big Pot of Simmered Meat

The Mexican kitchen traditionally simmers big chunks of meat, which gives two meals in one: tender boiled meat for tacos or enchiladas, as well as a hearty rich stock for soups and rice.

Serves 4

INGREDIENTS

4 lb. 8 oz. beef, pork, chicken
  for stewing any combination or
  just one type
2 onions, chopped
1 whole garlic bulb, cloves divided and
  peeled

several sprigs of fresh herbs, such
  as parsley, oregano, cilantro
1 carrot, sliced
1–2 stock cubes
salt and pepper

TO SERVE:
cooked thin noodles, to serve
finely sliced scallions, to garnish

1 Place the meat in a large pan and cover with cold water. Bring to a boil and skim any fat off the surface. Reduce the heat and add the onion, garlic, herbs, and carrot. Simmer, covered, for about 1 hour.

2 Add the stock cubes and salt and pepper to taste, then add the chicken (or whichever meat you prefer) and continue to simmer over a very low heat for about 2 hours until the meat is very tender.

3 Remove from the heat and allow the meat to cool in the stock. Transfer the meat to a bowl and shred; set aside. Skim the fat from the stock, or leave to chill then remove the fat by simply lifting it off of the soup. Strain the soup for a clearer soup. Reheat before serving.

4 To serve, spoon the hot macaroni or noodles into soup bowls, then top with the shredded meat and ladle over the soup. Garnish with scallions and serve.

VARIATIONS

For a simple soup to make from the strained stock, cook diced zucchini in the stock with a cinnamon stick; remove and discard the cinnamon stick, then serve the soup with a wedge of lime, a dash of salsa to taste, and a sprinkling of fresh cilantro.

Beef & Vegetable Soup

A wonderful meal-in-a-bowl, this soup is ideal for a winter supper or lunch.
The beefy flavor, enhanced with spices, is very warming.

Serves 4

INGREDIENTS

8 oz. tomatoes
2 ears of corn
4 cups beef soup or stock, following
   the recipe on page 22, or use a
   chilled ready-made stock
1 carrot, thinly sliced
1 onion, chopped

1–2 small waxy potatoes, diced
¼ cabbage, thinly sliced
¼ tsp. ground cumin
¼ tsp. mild chili powder
¼ tsp. paprika
8 oz. cooked beef (simmered in stock
   as in the recipe on page 22), cut

into bite-sized pieces
3–4 tbsp. chopped fresh cilantro
hot salsa, such as Scorched Chilli
   Salsa (see page 102), to serve

1 To skin the tomatoes, place in a heatproof bowl, pour boiling water over to cover and stand for 30 seconds. Drain and plunge into cold water. The skins will then slide off easily. Chop the skinned tomatoes.

2 Using a large knife, cut the ears of corn into 1-inch thick rounds.

3 Place the stock in a pan with the tomatoes, carrot, onion, potatoes, and cabbage. Bring to a boil, then reduce the heat and simmer for 10–15 minutes or until the vegetables are tender.

4 Add the corn-on-the-cob pieces, the cumin, chili powder, paprika, and beef pieces. Bring back to a boil over a medium heat.

5 Ladle into soup bowls and serve sprinkled with fresh cilantro, if using, with salsa handed round separately.

COOK'S TIP

To thicken the soup and give it a flavor of the popular Mexican steamed dumplings, known as a tamale, add a few tablespoons of masa harina, mixed into a thinnish paste with a little water, at Step 4. Stir well, then continue cooking until thickened.

Pozole

The dish of hulled maize kernels—hominy—simmered in rich stock is eaten all over Mexico, and is served with lots of fresh garnishes: shredded cabbage, onion, chilies, fried tortilla or crisp fried pork skin (chicharrones), and of course, chilies and lime wedges.

Serves 4

INGREDIENTS

1 lb. pork for stewing, such as lean
  belly
½ small chicken
about 8 cups water
1 chicken stock cube
1 whole garlic bulb, divided into
  cloves but not peeled

1 onion, chopped
2 bay leaves
1 lb. cooked hominy
¼–½ tsp. ground cumin
salt and pepper

TO SERVE:
½ small to medium cabbage, thinly
  sliced
dried oregano leaves
dried chili flakes
tortilla chips
lime wedges

1 Place the pork and chicken in a large pan. Add enough water to fill the pan. (Do not worry about having too much stock—it keeps fresh up to a week, and freezes well.)

2 Bring to a boil, then skim off the fat that rises to the surface. Reduce the heat and add the stock cube, garlic, onion, and bay leaves. Simmer, covered, over a medium-low heat until the pork and chicken are tender and cooked through.

3 Remove the pork and chicken from the soup and leave to cool. When cool enough to handle, remove the chicken flesh from the bones and cut the pork into bite-sized pieces. Set aside.

4 Skim the fat off the soup and discard the bay leaves. Add the hominy and cumin, salt and pepper to taste. Bring to a boil.

5 To serve, place a little pork and chicken in soup bowls. Top with cabbage, oregano, and chili flakes, then spoon in the hot soup. Serve with tortilla chips and lime.

Mexican Guacamole

Guacamole is at its best when freshly made, with enough texture to really taste the avocado.
Serve as a sauce for anything Mexican, or dip into it with vegetable sticks or tortilla chips.

Serves 4

INGREDIENTS

1 ripe tomato
2 limes
2–3 ripe small to medium avocados,
    or 1–2 large ones
¼–½ onion, finely chopped

pinch of ground cumin
pinch of mild chili powder
½–1 fresh green chilies, such as
    jalapeño or serrano, deseeded and
    finely chopped

1 tbsp. finely chopped fresh cilantro
    leaves, plus extra for garnishing
salt (optional)
tortilla chips, to serve (optional)

1 To skin the tomato, place in a heatproof bowl, pour boiling water over to cover and stand for 30 seconds. Drain and plunge into cold water. The skins will then slide off easily. Cut in half, deseed and chop the flesh.

2 Squeeze the juice from the limes into a bowl. Cut each avocado in half around the pit. Twist apart, then remove the pit with a knife. Carefully peel off the skin, dice the flesh, and toss in the bowl of lime juice to prevent discoloration. Repeat with the remaining avocados. Mash the avocados coarsely.

3 Add the onion, tomato, cumin, chili powder, chilies, and fresh cilantro to the avocados. If using as a dip for tortilla chips do not add salt. If using as a sauce, add salt to taste.

4 To serve as a dip, transfer to a serving dish, garnish with cilantro and serve with tortilla chips.

COOK'S TIP
Avocados grow in abundance in Mexico, and Guacamole is used to add richness and flavor to all manner of dishes. Try spooning it into soups, especially chicken or seafood, or spreading it into sandwiches on thick crusty rolls (tortas). Spoon guacamole over refried beans and melted cheese, then dig into it with salsa and crisp tortilla chips. Try serving guacamole with roasted chicken, or stirring it into the pan juices for a rich avocado sauce.

Roasted Cheese with Salsa

The combination of melting cheese and hot salsa is completely irresistible!
Called queso fundito in Mexico, it is often prepared on the barbecue
to nibble on while you wait for the rest of the meal to cook.

Serves 4

INGREDIENTS

8 oz. mozzarella, fresh pecorino or
Mexican queso oaxaca

$^2/_3$ cup Classic Tomato Salsa (see page
96), or other good salsa

½–1 onion, finely chopped
8 soft corn tortillas, to serve

1 To warm the corn tortillas ready for serving, heat a nonstick frying pan, add a tortilla and heat through, sprinkling with a few drops of water as it heats. Wrap in kitchen foil to keep warm. Repeat with the remaining tortillas.

2 Cut chunks or slabs of the cheese and arrange in a shallow ovenproof dish or in individual dishes.

3 Spoon the salsa over the cheese to cover and place in either a preheated oven at 400° F

or under a preheated broiler. Cook until the cheese melts and bubbles, lightly browning in spots.

4 Sprinkle with chopped onion to taste and serve with the warmed tortillas for dipping. Serve immediately as the melted cheese turns stringy when cold and becomes difficult to eat.

COOK'S TIP

Queso oaxaca is the authentic cheese to use, but mozzarella or pecorino make excellent substitutes since they produce the right effect when melted.

VARIATIONS

Use Salsa Verde (see page 96) in place of the red tomato salsa, and serve tortilla chips for dipping rather than soft corn tortillas.

Seafood Cocktail a la Veracruz

"Mariscos!" cry the signs in brightly painted colors along Mexico's beaches and sea fronts, wherever fresh seafood is served. This is a typical salad dish you might find there, full of spicy flavors.

Serves 6

INGREDIENTS

4 cups fish stock or water mixed
   with 1 fish stock cube
2 bay leaves
1 onion, chopped
3-5 garlic cloves, cut into big chunks
1 lb. 8 oz. mixed seafood, such as

shrimp in their shells, scallops,
   squid rings, pieces of squid
   tentacles, etc
¾ cup tomato ketchup
¼ cup Mexican hot sauce
generous pinch of ground cumin

6-8 tbsp. chopped fresh cilantro
4 tbsp. lime juice, plus extra for
   tossing
salt
1 avocado, to garnish

1 Place stock in a pan and add the bay leaves, half the onion, and all of the garlic. Bring to a boil, then simmer for about 10 minutes or until the onions are soft and the stock tastes flavorful.

2 Add the seafood in the order of the amount of cooking time required. Most small pieces of shellfish take a very short time to cook, and can be added together. Cook for 1 minute, remove from the heat and allow the seafood to finish cooking in the cooling stock.

3 When the stock has cooled, remove the seafood from the stock with a slotted spoon. Shell the shrimp and any other shellfish. Reserve the stock.

4 Combine the ketchup, hot sauce, and cumin in a bowl, reserving a quarter of the sauce mixture for serving. Add the seafood to the bowl with the remaining onion, fresh cilantro, lime juice, and about 1 cup of the reserved cooled fish stock. Stir carefully to mix and season.

5 Cut each avocado in half around the pit. Twist apart, then remove the pit with a knife. Carefully peel off the skin, then dice or slice the flesh. Toss in lime juice to prevent discoloration.

6 Serve the seafood cocktail in individual bowls, garnished with the avocado, and topped with a spoonful of the reserved sauce.

Citrus-marinated Fish

Ceviche, as it is called in Mexican, is one of Mexico's classic dishes: raw fish, cured in a bath of citrus juices, chilies, and aromatics. It must be made with the freshest fish to be sublime.

Serves 4

INGREDIENTS

1 lb. white-fleshed fish fillets, cut into bite-sized chunks
juice of 6–8 limes
2–3 ripe flavorful tomatoes, diced

3 fresh green chilies, such as jalapeño or serrano, deseeded and thinly sliced
½ tsp. dried oregano

⅓ cup extra-virgin olive oil
1 small onion, finely chopped
salt and pepper

1 Place the fish in nonmetallic dish, add the lime juice and mix well. Marinate in the refrigerator for 5 hours, or until the mixture looks opaque. Turn from time to time so that the lime juice permeates the fish.

2 An hour before serving, add the tomatoes, chilies, oregano, olive oil, and onion, then season with salt and pepper to taste.

3. About 15 minutes before serving, remove from the refrigerator so that the olive oil comes to room temperature.

Serve sprinkled with fresh cilantro.

COOK'S TIP

This dish makes an elegant starter served layered with rounds of crisp tortillas, like a stacked tostada. Or it makes a refreshing lunch, served piled up in halved avocados, surrounded by sliced mango, papaya, or grapefruit

COOK'S TIP

In this salad the fish is 'cooked' by the lime juice—do not leave too long otherwise the texture will spoil.

VARIATIONS

Serve garnished with marinated artichoke hearts, drained, either from a can or jar.

Salpicon of Crab

This lightly spiced crab salad is a cooling treat for a hot day. Eat it with crisp tortilla chips, or wrapped in a tender warm corn tortilla.

Serves 4

INGREDIENTS

¼ red onion, chopped
½–1 fresh green chili, deseeded and
   chopped
juice of ½ lime
1 tbsp. cider or other fruit vinegar,
   such as raspberry

1 tbsp. chopped fresh cilantro
1 tbsp. extra-virgin olive oil
8–12 oz. fresh crab meat
lettuce leave, to serve

GARNISH:
1 avocado
lime juice, for tossing
1–2 ripe tomatoes
3–5 radishes

1 Combine the onion, with the chili, lime juice, vinegar, fresh cilantro, and olive oil. Add the crab meat and toss lightly together.

2 To make the garnish, cut each avocado in half around the pit. Twist apart, then remove the pit with a knife. Carefully peel off the skin and slice the flesh. Toss gently in lime juice to prevent discoloration.

3 Halve the tomatoes, then remove the cores and seeds. Dice the flesh. Slice the radishes thinly.

4 Arrange the crab salad on a bed of lettuce leaves, garnish with the avocado, tomatoes, and radishes and serve at once.

VARIATIONS

For a toasted crab salad sandwich, split open a long roll or baguette and heap on crab salad. Top with a layer of cheese. Place the open roll under the broiler to heat through and melt the cheese. Spread the toasted plain side with a little mayonnaise and close the sandwich up. Cut and serve with some salsa.

Pickled Cauliflower, Carrots, & Chilies

In Mexican cantinas, these pickled vegetables are munched alongside a stack of warm buttered tortillas and washed down with glasses of chilled beer, or maybe a little shot of tequila and a wedge of lime.

Serves 6 as a relish

INGREDIENTS

3 tbsp. vegetable oil
1 onion, thinly sliced
5 garlic cloves, cut into slivers
3 carrots, thinly sliced
2 fresh green chilies, such as jalapeño or serrano, deseeded and cut into strips

1 small cauliflower, broken into florets or cut into bite-sized chunks
½ red bell pepper, cored, deseeded and diced or cut into strips
1 stalk celery, cut into bite-sized pieces

½ tsp. oregano leaves
1 bay leaf
¼ tsp. ground cumin
⅓ cup cider vinegar
salt and pepper

1 Heat the oil in a heavy frying pan and lightly sauté the onion, garlic, carrots, chilies, cauliflower, red bell pepper, and celery for about a minute.

2 Add the oregano, bay leaf, cumin, vinegar, and salt and pepper to taste. Add enough water to just cover the vegetables. Cook for a further 5–10 minutes or just

long enough for the vegetables to be tender but still firm to the bite.

3 Adjust the seasoning, adding more vinegar if needed. Leave to cool and serve as a relish. The mixture will keep for up to 2 weeks, covered, in the refrigerator.

COOK'S TIP

Wear rubber gloves when slicing and deseeding fresh chilies and do not touch your eyes during preparation.

Cheese & Bean Quesadillas

These bite-sized rolls are made from flour tortillas filled with a scrumptious mixture of refried beans, melted cheese, fresh cilantro, and salsa.

Serves 4-6

INGREDIENTS

8 flour tortillas
½ quantity Mexican Refried Beans
  (see page146) or refried beans
  (see page 144)

7 oz. cheddar cheese, grated
1 onion, chopped
½ bunch fresh cilantro leaves,
  chopped

1 quantity Salsa Cruda (see page 96)

1 First make the tortillas pliable, by warming them in a lightly greased nonstick frying pan.

2 Remove the tortillas from the pan and quickly spread with a layer of warm beans. Top each tortilla with grated cheese, onion, fresh cilantro, and a spoonful of salsa. Roll up tightly.

3 Just before serving, heat the nonstick frying pan over a medium heat, sprinkling lightly with a drop or two of water. Add the tortilla rolls, cover the pan and heat through until the cheese melts. Allow to lightly brown, if wished.

4 Remove from the pan and slice each roll, on the diagonal, into about 4 bite-sized pieces. Serve at once.

VARIATIONS

Top each tortilla with florets of lightly cooked broccoli or sautéed sliced wild mushrooms instead of the beans, for a more lightweight filling.

VARIATION

Cooked drained black beans can also be substituted for the refried beans. Use with Chipotle Salsa (see page 100) instead of the Salsa Cruda for a subtle change of flavor.

COOK'S TIP

Flour tortillas can also be warmed in the microwave, but take care not to heat them for too long as they can become leathery.

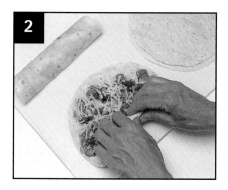

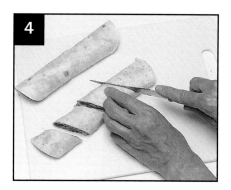

Chorizo & Artichoke Heart Quesadillas

Ideal to serve with drinks, these appetizers are incredibly easy to make—simply top flat tortillas with a delicious filling, pop under the broiler, then serve in wedges.

Serves 4-6

INGREDIENTS

1 chorizo sausage
1 large mild green chili or green bell pepper (optional)
8–10 marinated artichoke hearts or

canned artichoke hearts, drained and diced
2 garlic cloves, finely chopped
4 soft corn tortillas, warmed

12 oz. grated cheese
1 tomato, diced
2 scallions, thinly sliced
1 tbsp. chopped fresh cilantro

1 Dice the chorizo sausage. Heat a heavy-based frying pan, add the chorizo and fry until it browns in places.

2 If using the mild chili or bell pepper, place under a preheated hot broiler and broil for about 10 minutes, or until the skins are charred and the flesh softened. Place in a plastic bag, twist to seal and set aside for 20 minutes. Remove the

skins with a knife, then deseed and chop.

3 Arrange the browned chorizo and artichoke hearts on the corn tortillas, then transfer half to a baking sheet.

4 Sprinkle with the garlic, then the cheese. Place under a preheated hot broiler and broil until the cheese melts and sizzles. Repeat with the remaining tortillas.

5 Sprinkle with the diced tomato, scallions, green chili, or bell pepper, if using, and fresh cilantro. Cut into wedges and serve.

Spicy Shrimp & Avocado on Crisp Tortilla Wedges

A winning combination of textures and flavors, spiced shrimp and creamy avocado are served on crisply fried tortilla wedges to make a palate-pleasing appetizer.

Serves 8-10

INGREDIENTS

1 lb. cooked shrimp
4 garlic cloves, finely chopped
½ tsp. mild chili powder
½ tsp. ground cumin

juice of 1 lime
1 ripe tomato, diced
salt
6 soft corn tortillas

vegetable oil, for frying
2 avocados
3/4 cup sour cream
mild chili powder, to garnish

1 Place the shrimp in a bowl with the garlic, chili powder, cumin, lime juice, and tomato. Add salt to taste and stir gently to mix. Chill for at least 4 hours or overnight to allow the flavors to mingle.

2 Cut the tortillas into wedges. Heat a little oil in a nonstick frying pan, add a batch of tortilla wedges and fry over a medium heat until crisp. Repeat with the remaining wedges and transfer to a serving platter.

3 Cut each avocado in half around the pit. Twist apart, then remove the pit with a knife. Carefully peel off the skin and dice the flesh. Gently stir into the shrimp mixture.

4 Top each tortilla wedge with a small mound of the shrimp and avocado mixture. Finish with a dab of sour cream, garnish with a light sprinkling of chili powder and serve.

COOK'S TIP

For speed, you can use crisp corn tortillas (tostadas) or nacho chips (get the unsalted kind) instead of the corn tortillas.

VARIATIONS

Substitute diced mozzarella or mild fresh pecorino for the shrimp and marinate for a few hours.

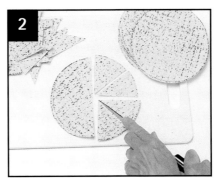

Black Bean Nachos

Packed with authentic Mexican flavors, this tasty black bean and cheese dip is fun to eat and will get any meal off to a good start! As an added bonus, it takes mere minutes to put together.

Serves 4

INGREDIENTS

1 cup dried black beans, or canned
   black beans, drained
6-8 oz. grated cheese, such as
   cheddar, Fontina, pecorino, asiago,
   or a combination

about ¼ tsp. cumin seeds or
   ground cumin
about 4 tbsp. sour cream
thinly sliced pickled jalapeños
   (optional)

1 tbsp. chopped fresh cilantro
handful of shredded lettuce
tortilla chips, to serve

1 If using dried black beans, soak the beans overnight, then drain. Put in a pan, cover with water and bring to a boil. Boil for 10 minutes, then reduce the heat and simmer for about 1½ hours until tender. Drain well.

2 Spread the beans in a shallow ovenproof dish, then scatter the cheese over the top. Sprinkle with cumin, to taste.

3 Bake in a preheated oven at 375° F for 10–15 minutes or until the cheese is bubbly and melted.

4 Remove the beans and cheese from the oven and spoon the sour cream on top. Add the jalapeños, if using, and sprinkle with fresh cilantro and lettuce.

5 Arrange the tortilla chips around the beans, sticking them into the mixture. Serve at once.

VARIATIONS

To add a meaty flavor, spoon chopped and browned chorizo on top of the beans, before adding the cheese, and cook as in Step 3—the combination is excellent. Finely chopped leftover cooked meat can also be added in this way.

Refried Bean Nachos

*A Mexican classic, refried beans and tortilla crisps are topped
with luscious melted cheese, salsa, and assorted toppings, to make an irresistible dip.
Perfect for an informal gathering!*

Serves 6-8

INGREDIENTS

14 oz. refried beans
14 oz. can pinto beans, drained
large pinch of ground cumin
large pinch of mild chili powder
6 oz. bag tortilla chips

8 oz. grated cheese, such as cheddar
salsa of your choice
1 avocado, pitted, diced
  and tossed with lime juice
½ small onion or 3-5 scallions,

chopped
2 ripe tomatoes, diced
handful of shredded lettuce
3-4 tbsp. chopped fresh cilantro
sour cream, to serve

1 Place the refried beans in a pan with the pinto beans, cumin, and chili powder. Add enough water to make a thick soup-like consistency, stirring gently so that the beans do not lose their texture.

2 Heat the bean mixture over a medium heat until hot, then reduce the heat and keep warm while you prepare the rest of the dish.

3 Arrange half the tortilla chips in the bottom of a flameproof casserole or gratin dish and cover with the bean mixture. Sprinkle with the cheese and bake in a preheated oven at 400° F until the cheese melts. Alternatively, place the casserole under the broiler and broil for 5-7 minutes or until the cheese melts and lightly sizzles in places.

4 Arrange on top of the melted cheese the salsa, avocado, onion, tomato, lettuce, and fresh cilantro. Surround with the remaining tortilla chips and serve immediately, accompanied by sour cream.

VARIATIONS

Try watercress and yogurt instead of lettuce and sour cream, respectively.

Sincronizadas

Once you've tried this Mexican version of a toasted ham and cheese sandwich, you'll never look back! Serve with a tangy salsa and Mexican beer to complete the snack.

Serves 6

INGREDIENTS

vegetable oil, for greasing
about 10 flour tortillas

1 lb. grated cheese
8 oz. cooked ham, diced

salsa of your choice
sour cream with herbs, to serve

1 Lightly grease a nonstick frying pan. Off the heat, place one tortilla in the pan and top with a layer of cheese and ham. Generously spread salsa over another tortilla and place, salsa-side down, on top of the cheese and ham tortilla in the pan.

2 Place over a medium heat and cook until the cheese is melted and the base of the tortilla is golden brown.

3 Place a heatproof plate, upside-down, on top of the pan. Taking care to protect your hands, hold the plate firmly in place and carefully invert the pan to turn the "sandwich" out onto the plate. Slide the "sandwich" back into the pan and cook until the underside of the tortilla is golden brown.

4 Remove from the pan and serve cut into wedges, accompanied by sour cream.

VARIATIONS

For a vegetarian version, sauté 8 oz. sliced mushrooms in a little olive oil with a crushed garlic clove and use instead of the ham. Alternatively, lightly fry finely chopped garlic in a little oil, then add rinsed spinach leaves and cook until wilted; chop and substitute for the ham.

COOK'S TIP

Protect your hands with oven mitts when turning the tortillas on to the plate.

Tortas

Throughout Mexico you will find street vendors selling these substantial Mexican rolls.
Filled with all sorts of ingredients, they are "muy delicioso!"
Make your own and vary the filling as you wish.

Serves 4

INGREDIENTS

4 crusty rolls, such as French rolls or
   bocadillos
melted butter or olive oil, for brushing
1 cup refried beans (see page 144)
1½ cups shredded cooked chicken,
   browned chorizo pieces, sliced ham

and cheese or any leftover cooked
   meat you have to hand
1 ripe tomato, sliced or diced
1 small onion, finely chopped
2 tbsp. chopped fresh cilantro
1 avocado, pitted, sliced and tossed

with lime juice
4-6 tbsp. sour cream
salsa of your choice
handful of shredded lettuce

1 Cut the rolls in half and remove a little of the crumb to make space for the filling.

2 Brush the outside and inside of the rolls with butter or oil and toast, on both sides, on a hot griddle or frying pan for a few minutes until crisp. Alternatively, place in a preheated oven at 400° F until lightly toasted.

3 Meanwhile, place the beans in a pan with a tiny amount of water and heat through gently.

4 When the rolls are heated, spread one half of each roll generously with the beans, then top with a layer of cooked meat. Top with tomato, onion, fresh cilantro, and avocado.

5 Generously spread sour cream onto the other side of each

roll. Drizzle the salsa over the filling, add a little shredded lettuce, then sandwich the two sides of each roll together; press tightly. Serve immediately.

VARIATIONS

Add any Mexican sauce, such as Chile Verde (see page 204), to the meat filling to vary the flavor.

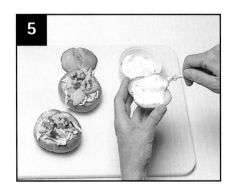

Molletes

Molletes are crusty rolls stuffed with hot melted beans and cheese, then garnished with a tangy hot salsa. In this version, a spicy shredded cabbage salad adds extra crunch to the snacks.

Serves 4

INGREDIENTS

4 bread rolls

1 tbsp. vegetable oil, plus extra for brushing

14 oz. can refried beans

1 onion, chopped

3 garlic cloves, chopped

3 slices bacon, cut into small pieces,

or about 3 oz. spicy chorizo, diced

8 oz. diced fresh or canned tomatoes

¼–½ tsp. ground cumin

9 oz. grated cheese

CABBAGE SALAD:

½ cabbage, thinly sliced

2 tbsp. sliced pickled jalapeños from a jar

1 tbsp. extra-virgin olive oil

3 tbsp. cider vinegar

¼ tsp. dried oregano

salt and pepper

1 Cut the rolls in half and remove a little of the crumb to make space for the filling.

2 To make the cabbage salad, combine the cabbage with the jalapeños, olive oil, and vinegar. Season with salt, pepper and oregano. Set aside.

3 Brush the rolls all over with oil. Arrange on a baking sheet and toast in a preheated oven at

400° F oven for 10–15 minutes until the rolls are crisp and light golden.

4 Meanwhile, place the beans in a pan and heat through gently with enough water to thin them to a smooth paste.

5 Heat 1 tablespoon of the oil in a frying pan. Add the onion, garlic and bacon or chorizo and cook until the bacon or chorizo is

browned and the onion softened. Add the tomatoes and simmer, stirring, until they break down to form a thick sauce.

6 Add the beans to the frying pan and stir to combine with the onion mixture. Stir in the cumin, to taste. Set aside.

7 Remove the rolls from the oven: keep the oven on. Fill the rolls with the warm bean mixture, then top with the cheese and close up tightly. Return to the baking sheet and heat through in the oven until the cheese melts.

8 Open the rolls up and spoon in a little cabbage salad. Serve immediately.

Spicy-sweet Meat Empanadas

This is a great make-ahead appetizer as it can be frozen for a month, then just popped into the oven at the last moment—they will still taste marvelous!

Serves 4-6

INGREDIENTS

12 oz. puff pastry
all-purpose flour, for dusting
1 quantity Picadillo (see page 198)

1 egg yolk, beaten with 1-2 tbsp.
water

TO SERVE:
green olives
mixed chilies

1 Roll out the puff pastry into a thin layer on a lightly floured surface. Using a 6 inch cutter, cut the pastry into 8 rounds.

2 Place a tablespoon or two of the filling in the middle of one round.

3 Brush the edge of the pastry with beaten egg, then fold in half and press the edges to seal. Press the tines of a fork along the sealed edges to make the seal more secure. Prick the top of the empanada with the fork, then place on a baking sheet. Brush with beaten egg. Repeat with the remaining pastry rounds and filling.

4 Bake the empanadas in a preheated oven at 375° F for 15–25 minutes or until golden on the outside and hot in the middle.

5 Serve immediately, hot and sizzling from the oven, accompanied by a bowl of olives and chilies.

VARIATIONS

For chicken empanadas, replace the Picadillo with diced cooked chicken, flavored with some mild chili sauce.

VARIATIONS

For vegetarian empanadas, replace the filling with a mixture of diced Gouda or cheddar cheese, chopped onion, fresh cilantro, cumin seeds, and sliced pimiento-stuffed green olives. Fill and bake as described.

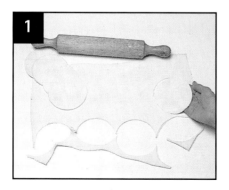

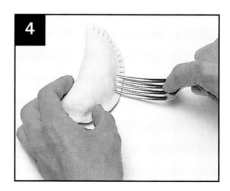

Masa Tartlets with Beans & Avocado

Packed with Mexican flavors, these little golden tartlets make a colorful start to a meal or a tasty light lunch, when served with mixed salad leaves.

Serves 4

INGREDIENTS

8-10 tbsp. masa harina
3 tbsp. all purpose flour
pinch of baking soda
1 cup warm water
vegetable oil, for frying
1 cup pinto beans or refried beans

(see page 144), heated through
1 avocado, pitted, sliced and tossed
with lime juice
3 oz. queso fresco or fresh cream
cheese or crumbled feta
salsa of your choice

2 scallions, thinly sliced

TO GARNISH:
fresh flat-leaf parsley sprigs
lemon wedges

1 Mix the masa harina with the all-purpose flour and baking soda in a bowl, then mix in enough warm water to make a firm yet moist dough.

2 Pinch off about a walnut-sized piece of dough and, using your fingers, shape into a tiny tartlet shape, pressing and pinching to make it as thin as possible without falling apart. Repeat with the remaining dough.

3 Heat a layer of oil in a deep frying pan until it is smoking. Add a batch of tartlets to the hot oil and fry, spooning the hot fat into the center of the tartlets and turning once, until golden on all sides.

4 Using a slotted spoon, remove the tartlets from the hot oil and drain on paper towels. Place on a baking sheet and keep warm in a low oven, while cooking the remaining tartlets.

5 To serve, fill each tartlet shell with the warmed beans, avocado, cheese, salsa, and scallions. Garnish with parsley and lemon wedges and serve at once.

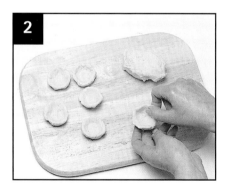

Salads, Side Dishes, & Sauces

Salads of crisp raw vegetables and fruits, often eaten piled on top of richer savory cooked dishes, such as enchiladas or barbecued food, are full of strong fresh flavor and rich with vitamins, too. Pomegranate, papaya, and tangy citrus fruits are combined with avocado or red bell peppers to stunning effect.

For heartier salads, Steak, Avocado, and Bean Salad is sure to satisfy, while summer squash and chorizo, two popular ingredients in Mexico, make the basis for a great lunch-time snack.

Potatoes are given the Mexican treatment, coated in a rich goat's cheese and smoky chili sauce, and for a classic side dish try fragrant Roasted Green Chilies in Cumin-Garlic Cream.

Sauces for topping meat and fish or for filling tortillas are on offer in this chapter, too—the Quick Tomato Sauce can be used for all manner of dishes, while Hot Sauce of Dried Chilies will add a hotnesss that is the very essence of Mexican cuisine. Mole Polbano, the classic sauce of chilies and chocolate, is not to be missed.

Papaya, Avocado, & Red Bell Pepper Salad

This colorful and refreshing salad, with its sweet and spicy flavors, is the perfect foil to a meaty main dish, and is particularly good with barbecue.

Serves 4–6

INGREDIENTS

7 oz. mixed green salad leaves
2-3 scallions, chopped
3-4 tbsp. chopped fresh cilantro
1 small papaya
2 red bell peppers
1 avocado
1 tbsp. lime juice

3-4 tbsp. pumpkin seeds, preferably
  toasted (optional)

DRESSING:
juice of 1 lime
large pinch of paprika,
large pinch of ground cumin

large pinch of sugar
1 garlic clove, finely chopped
4 tbsp. extra-virgin olive oil
dash of white wine vinegar (optional)
salt

1 Combine the salad leaves with the scallions and cilantro. Transfer to a serving dish.

2 Cut the papaya in half and scoop out the seeds with a spoon. Cut into quarters, remove the peel and slice the flesh. Arrange on top of the salad leaves. Cut the bell peppers in half, remove the cores and seeds, then slice thinly. Add to the salad leaves.

3 Cut the avocado in half around the pit. Twist apart, then remove the pit with a knife. Carefully peel off the skin, dice the flesh and toss in lime juice to prevent discoloration. Add to the other salad ingredients.

4 To make the dressing, whisk together the lime juice, paprika, ground cumin, sugar, garlic and olive oil. Add salt to taste.

5 Pour the dressing over the salad and toss lightly, adding a dash of wine vinegar if a flavor with more 'bite' is preferred. Sprinkle with the toasted pumpkin seeds, if using.

Green Bean Salad with Feta Cheese

This fresh-tasting salad is flavored with fresh cilantro, a herb used widely in Mexican cooking.

Serves 4

INGREDIENTS

12 oz. green beans, topped and tailed

1 red onion, chopped

3-4 tbsp. chopped fresh cilantro

2 radishes, thinly sliced

2 3/4 oz. feta cheese, crumbled

1 tsp. chopped fresh oregano or ½ tsp. dried

2 tbsp. red wine or fruit vinegar

$^1/_3$ cup extra-virgin olive oil

3 ripe tomatoes, cut into wedges

pepper

1 Bring about 2 inches water to a boil in the bottom of a steamer. Add the beans to the top part of the steamer, cover, and steam for about 5 minutes until just tender.

2 Put the beans in a bowl and add the onion, cilantro, radishes, and feta cheese.

3 Sprinkle the oregano over the salad, then grind pepper over to taste. Mix the vinegar and olive oil together and pour over the salad. Toss gently to mix well.

4 Transfer to a serving platter, surround with the tomato wedges and serve at once, or chill until ready to serve.

VARIATIONS

This recipe is also delicious made with nopales, or edible cactus, which is used as a vegetable in Mexican cooking. It is available in specialty stores in cans or jars. Simply drain the cactus, then slice and use instead of the green beans, missing out Step 1. When using cactus, replace the feta cheese with 1-2 chopped hard-boiled eggs, or add 2 roasted very mild green chilies, sliced.

Citrus Salad
with Pomegranate & Avocado

*A salad like this reminds us of how much Mexico and the Mediterranean
share in terms of sunny flavors and ingredients.*

Serves 4

INGREDIENTS

1 large pomegranate
1 grapefruit
2 sweet oranges
finely grated rind of ½ lime
1-2 garlic cloves, finely chopped
3 tbsp. red wine vinegar

juice of 2 limes
½ tsp. sugar
¼ tsp. dry mustard
4-5 tbsp. extra-virgin olive oil
1 head red leafy lettuce, such as
   oakleaf, washed and dried

1 avocado, pitted, diced and tossed
   with a little lime juice
salt and pepper
½ red onion, thinly sliced, to garnish

1 Cut the pomegranate into quarters, then press back the outer skin to push out the seeds into a bowl.

2 Using a sharp knife, cut a slice off the top and bottom of the grapefruit, then remove the peel and pith, cutting downward. Cut out the segments from between the membranes, then add to the pomegranate.

3 Finely grate the rind of half an orange and set aside. Using a sharp knife, cut a slice off the top and bottom of both oranges, then remove the peel and pith, cutting downward and taking care to retain the shape of the oranges. Slice horizontally into slices, then cut into quarters. Add to the pomegranate and grapefruit and stir to mix well.

4 Combine the reserved orange rind with the lime rind, garlic, vinegar, lime juice, sugar, and mustard. Season with salt and pepper, then whisk in the olive oil.

5 Place the lettuce leaves in a serving bowl, top with the citrus mixture and avocado. Pour over the dressing and toss. Garnish with onion rings and serve at once.

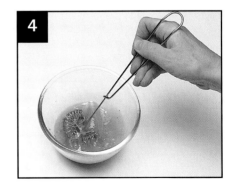

Zucchini & Tomatoes with Green Chili Vinaigrette

Lightly cooked zucchini are mixed with ripe, juicy tomatoes and dressed with a chili vinaigrette to create a perfect side salad for a summer lunch or supper.

Serves 4–6

INGREDIENTS

1 large fresh mild green chili, or a combination of 1 green bell pepper and ½–1 fresh green chili
4 zucchini, sliced

4 ripe tomatoes, diced or sliced
2–3 garlic cloves, finely chopped
pinch sugar
¼ tsp. ground cumin

2 tbsp. white wine vinegar
4 tbsp. extra-virgin olive oil
2–3 tbsp. cilantro
salt and pepper

1 Roast the mild chili, or the combination of the green bell pepper and chili, in a heavy-based ungreased frying pan or under a preheated broiler until the skin is charred. Place in a plastic bag, twist to seal well and leave to stand for 20 minutes.

2 Peel the skin from the chili and bell pepper, if using, then remove the seeds and slice the flesh. Set aside.

3 Bring about 2 inches water to a boil in the bottom of a steamer. Add the zucchini to the top part of the steamer, cover and steam for about 5 minutes until just tender.

4 Combine the garlic, sugar, cumin, vinegar, olive oil, cilantro, and chili in a bowl, then season with salt and pepper to taste.

5 Arrange the zucchini and tomatoes in a serving bowl or on a platter and spoon over the chili dressing. Toss gently, if wished, and serve.

VARIATIONS

Add 8 oz. cooked peeled shrimp to the zucchini and tomatoes, then coat with the dressing as in Step 5.

Steak, Avocado, & Bean Salad

The Californian influence on Mexican food is evident in this big, hearty salad.
Packed with delicious ingredients, this fantastic dish is a meal in itself.

Serves 4

INGREDIENTS

12 oz. tender steak, such as sirloin

4 garlic cloves, chopped

juice of 1 lime

4 tbsp. extra-virgin olive oil

1 tbsp. white or red wine vinegar

¼ tsp. mild chili powder

¼ tsp. ground cumin

½ tsp. paprika

pinch of sugar (optional)

5 scallions, thinly sliced

about 7 oz. crisp lettuce leaves, such as romaine

14 oz. can pinto, black or red kidney beans

1 avocado, pitted, sliced and tossed with a little lime juice

2 ripe tomatoes, diced

¼ fresh green or red chili, chopped

3 tbsp. chopped fresh cilantro

8 oz. can corn, drained

generous handful of crisp tortilla chips, broken into pieces

salt and pepper

1 Place the steak in a nonmetallic dish with the garlic and half the lime and olive oil. Season with salt and pepper, then leave to marinate while you prepare the other ingredients.

2 To make the dressing, combine the remaining lime juice and olive oil with the vinegar, chili powder, cumin, and paprika. Add a pinch of sugar to taste. Set aside.

3 Pan-fry the steak, or cook under a preheated broiler, until browned on the outside and cooked to your liking in the middle. Remove from the pan, cut into strips and reserve: keep warm or allow to cool.

4 Toss the scallions with the lettuce and arrange on a serving platter. Pour about half the dressing over the leaves, then arrange the beans, avocado, and tomatoes over the top. Sprinkle with the chili, cilantro, and corn.

5 Arrange the steak and the tortilla chips on top, pour over the rest of the dressing, and serve immediately.

Zucchini & Summer Squash with Chorizo

*The spicy richness of chorizo marries well with zucchini and squash,
giving them a real flavor lift.*

Serves 4

INGREDIENTS

2 zucchini, thinly sliced

2 yellow summer squash, thinly sliced

2 fresh chorizo sausages, diced or
   sliced

3 garlic cloves, finely chopped

juice of ½-1 lime

1-2 tbsp. chopped fresh cilantro

salt and pepper

1 Cook the zucchini and summer squash in boiling salted water for 3-4 minutes until they are just tender, then drain well.

2 Brown the chorizo in a heavy-based frying pan, stirring with a spoon to break up into pieces. Pour off any excess fat from the browned chorizo.

3 Add the garlic and blanched zucchini and summer squash. Cook for a few minutes, stirring gently, to combine the flavors. Season with salt and pepper and serve sprinkled with cilantro.

COOK'S TIP

Mild in flavor and ideal for combining with spicy meats, squash is a favorite Mexican vegetable. If desired, this dish can be prepared with squash only—yellow pattypans would be ideal.

VARIATIONS

If available, use chayote or cho-cho squash, which is indigenous to Mexico. Pear-shaped and pale green, with a corrugated skin, chayote is crisp and delicately-flavored. To prepare, simply peel and slice, then blanch as in Step 1, cooking for a few minutes longer. Use with yellow summer squash for color.

Summer Squash with Green Chilies, Tomatoes, & Corn

Garlicky butter and a hint of chili flavor this summertime vegetable pot of squash and corn. Serve alongside almost any meaty main course, especially a roasted chicken; good, too with Fajitas.

Serves 4-6

INGREDIENTS

2 ears of corn

2 small zucchini or other green summer squash, such as pattypan, cubed or sliced

2 small yellow summer squash, cubed or sliced

2 tbsp. butter

3 garlic cloves, finely chopped

3-4 large, ripe flavorful tomatoes, diced

several pinches of mild chili powder

several pinches of ground cumin

½ fresh green chili, such as jalapeño, deseeded and chopped

pinch of sugar

salt and pepper

1 Bring about 2 inches water to a boil in the bottom of a steamer. Add the corn, zucchini, and summer squash to the top part of the steamer, cover and steam for about 3 minutes depending on their maturity and freshness. Alternatively, blanch in boiling salted water for about 3 minutes, then drain. Set aside until cool enough to handle.

2 Using a large knife, slice the corn kernels off the cob and set aside.

3 Melt the butter in a heavy-based frying pan. Add the garlic and cook for 1 minute to soften. Add the tomatoes, chili powder, ground cumin, green chili, and sugar to taste. Season with salt and pepper to taste and cook for a few minutes or until the flavors have mingled.

4 Add the corn kernels, zucchini, and squash. Cook for 2 minutes, stirring, to warm through. Serve immediately.

VARIATIONS

Any leftovers will make a good addition to, or base for, a lovely summer soup. Just add stock, cilantro, and some lime.

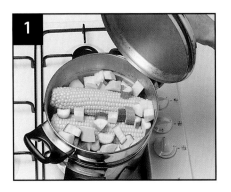

Potatoes in Salsa

*Earthy potatoes, served in the tangy spicy tomatillo sauce and topped with scallions and sour cream,
is delicious either as a side dish with simmered or braised meat,
or as a vegetarian main course.*

Serves 6

INGREDIENTS

2 lb. 4 oz. small waxy potatoes, peeled
1 onion, halved and unpeeled
8 garlic cloves, unpeeled
8 tomatillos, outer husks removed, or small tart tomatoes
1 fresh green chili

1 cup chicken, meat or vegetable stock (see Cook's Tip)
½ tsp. ground cumin
1 sprig fresh thyme or generous pinch dried
1 sprig fresh oregano or generous

pinch dried
2 tbsp. vegetable or extra-virgin olive oil
1 bunch cilantro, chopped
salt

1 Put the potatoes in a pan of salted water. Bring to a boil and cook for about 15 minutes or until almost tender. Do not over-cook them. Drain and set aside.

2 Lightly char the onion, garlic, chili, and tomatillos in a heavy-based ungreased frying pan. Set aside, and when cool enough to handle, peel and chop the onion, garlic, and chili; chop the

tomatillos or tomatoes. Put in a blender or food processor with half the stock and process to form a purée. Add the cumin, thyme, and oregano.

3 Heat the oil in a heavy-based frying pan. Add the purée and cook over a medium heat for about 5 minutes, stirring, to reduce slightly and concentrate the flavors.

4 Add the potatoes and zucchini and pour in the rest of the stock. Add about half the cilantro and cook for 5–10 minutes until the zucchini are tender.

5 Transfer to a serving bowl and serve sprinkled with the remaining cilantro.

Potatoes with Goat's Cheese & Chipotle Cream

This makes a luscious side dish to serve with meat, or a satisfying vegetarian main course. Goat's cheese is a traditional food of Mexico, and is enjoying great renewed popularity.

Serves 4

INGREDIENTS

2 lb. 12 oz. baking potatoes, peeled and cut into chunks
pinch of salt
pinch of sugar
7 fl oz. crème fraîche
4 fl oz. vegetable or chicken stock

3 garlic cloves, finely chopped
a few shakes of bottled chipotle salsa, or ½ dried chipotle, reconstituted (see page 100), deseeded and thinly sliced
8 oz. goat's cheese, sliced

6 oz. mozzarella or cheddar cheese, grated
⅔ cup Parmesan or pecorino cheese, grated
salt

1 Put the potatoes in a pan of water with the salt and sugar. Bring to a boil and cook for about 10 minutes until they are half cooked.

2 Combine the crème fraîche with the stock, garlic, and the chipotle salsa.

3 Arrange half the potatoes in a casserole. Pour half the crème fraîche sauce over the potatoes and cover with the goat's cheese. Top with the remaining potatoes and sauce.

4 Sprinkle with the grated mozzarella or cheddar cheese, then with the grated Parmesan or pecorino.

5 Bake in a preheated oven at 350° F until the potatoes are tender and the cheese topping is lightly golden and crisped in places. Serve immediately.

Roasted Green Chilies in Cumin-Garlic Cream

*Roasted mild green chilies are delicious simmered with cumin-scented cream.
It's important not to make this too hot, otherwise the fragrant aromas will be overpowered.*

Serves 4–6

INGREDIENTS

4 large fresh mild green chilies, such
    as anaheim or poblano, or a
    combination of 4 green bell peppers
    and 2 jalapeños
2 tbsp. butter

1 onion, finely chopped
3 garlic cloves, finely chopped
¼ tsp. ground cumin
1 cup light cream
1 cup chicken or vegetable stock

salt and pepper
1 lime, halved, to serve

1 Roast the mild chilies, or the combination of bell peppers and jalapeños, in a heavy-based ungreased frying pan or under a preheated broiler until the skins are charred. Place in a plastic bag, twist to seal well and leave to stand for 20 minutes to allow the skins to loosen.

2 Remove the seeds from the chilies and bell peppers, if using, and peel off the skins. Slice the flesh. Set aside.

3 Melt the butter in a large frying pan, add the onion and garlic and sauté for about 3 minutes until softened. Sprinkle with the cumin and season with salt and pepper to taste.

4 Stir in the sliced chilies and pour in the cream and stock. Cook over a medium heat, stirring, until the liquid reduces in volume and forms a richly flavored sauce.

5 Transfer to a serving dish and serve warm, squeezing over lime juice at the last minute.

VARIATIONS

Add an equal amount of corn with the chilies—it will add a delicious sweetness to the dish.

Quick Tomato Sauce

Simple to make, this versatile sauce is not only a great accompaniment for barbecued meat and fish, but also invaluable for baked tortilla dishes and taco fillings.

Serves 4-6

INGREDIENTS

2 tbsp. vegetable or olive oil
1 onion, thinly sliced
5 garlic cloves, thinly sliced

14 oz. can tomatoes, diced, plus their juices, or 1 lb. 5 oz. fresh diced tomatoes
several shakes of mild chili powder

1½ cups vegetable or chicken stock
salt and pepper
pinch of sugar (optional)

1 Heat the oil in a large frying pan. Add the onion and garlic and cook, stirring, until just softened.

2 Add the tomatoes, chili powder to taste, and the stock. Cook over a medium-high heat for about 10 minutes or until the tomatoes have reduced slightly and the flavor is more concentrated.

3 Season with salt, pepper, and sugar to taste and serve warm.

COOK'S TIP

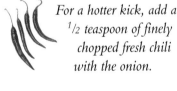

If using fresh tomatoes for this sauce, make sure they are very ripe and flavorful. Skin and deseed fresh tomatoes before dicing.

COOK'S TIP

The sauce will keep covered in the refrigerator for up to 3 days.

VARIATION

For a hotter kick, add a ½ teaspoon of finely chopped fresh chili with the onion.

Hot Tomato Sauce

This tangy sauce is excellent with crispy tortillas and tostadas,
or with grilled or fried fish. Try it with fish and chips for a change!

Serves 4

INGREDIENTS

2-3 fresh green chilies, such as
   jalapeño or serrano
8 oz. canned chopped
   tomatoes

1 scallion, thinly sliced
2 garlic cloves, chopped
2-3 tbsp. cider vinegar
1/4-1/3 cup water

large pinch of dried oregano
large pinch of ground cumin
large pinch of sugar
large pinch of salt

1 Slice the chilies open, remove the seeds if desired, then chop the chilies.

2 Put the chilies in a blender or food processor together with the tomatoes, scallion, garlic, vinegar, water, oregano, cumin, sugar, and salt. Process until smooth.

3 Adjust the seasoning and chill until ready to serve. The sauce will keep for up to a week, covered, in the refrigerator.

COOK'S TIP

If you have sensitive skin, it may be advisable to wear rubber gloves when preparing chilies, as the oil in the seeds and flesh can cause irritation. Make sure that you do not touch your eyes when handling cut chilies.

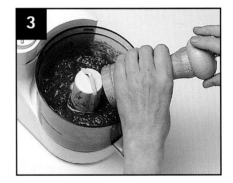

Mild Red Chili Sauce

This milder sauce is ideal for enchiladas and stewed meat. Keep some stashed in your freezer at all times, for an instant dash of Mexico!

Makes about 1 ½ cups

INGREDIENTS

5 large fresh mild chilies, such as New Mexico or ancho

2 cups vegetable or chicken stock

1 tbsp. masa harina or 1 crumbled

corn tortilla, puréed with enough water to make a thin paste

large pinch of ground cumin

1-2 garlic cloves, finely chopped

juice of 1 lime

salt

1 Using metal tongs, roast each chili over an open flame until the color darkens on all sides. Alternatively, place under a preheated broiler, turning them frequently. Do not allow to burn.

2 Put the chilies in a bowl and pour boiling water over them. Cover and leave to cool.

3 Meanwhile, put the stock in a pan and bring to a simmer.

4 When the chilies have cooled and are swelled up and softened, remove from the water with a slotted spoon. Remove the seeds from the chilies, then cut or tear the flesh into pieces and place in a blender or food processor. Process to form a purée, then mix in the hot stock.

5 Put the chili and stock mixture in a pan. Add the masa harina or puréed tortilla, cumin, garlic, and lime juice. Bring to a boil and cook for a few minutes, stirring,

until the sauce has thickened. Adjust the seasoning and serve.

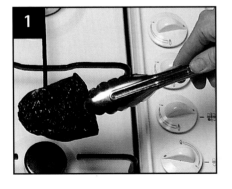

Hot Sauce of Dried Chilies

This hot smokey sauce is an excellent accompaniment to all kinds of roasted meats. Not for the faint of heart!

Makes about 1 cup

INGREDIENTS

10 dried arbol chilies, stems removed (see Cook's Tip)

1 cup cider or white wine vinegar
½ tsp. salt

1 Place the chilies in a mortar and crush finely with a pestle.

2 Put the vinegar in a pan and add the chilies and salt. Stir to combine, then bring to a boil.

3 Remove from the heat and leave to cool and infuse. Pour into a bowl and serve. The sauce will keep for up to a month, covered, in the refrigerator.

COOK'S TIP

Arbol are dried long hot red chilies, with a dusty heat that is reminiscent of the Mexican desert. If arbol chilies are not available, use any hot dried chili, or chili flakes, such as cayenne.

COOK'S TIP

Hot sauce can be bottled by pouring into sterilized jars and treating it as you would any long-keeping jam, jelly, or preserve.

Mole Poblano

This great Mexican celebration dish, ladled out at village fiestas, birthday parties, baptisms, and weddings, is known for its unusual combination of chilies and chocolate.

Serves 8–10

INGREDIENTS

3 fresh mulato chilies

3 fresh mild ancho chilies

5-6 fresh Anaheim chilies

1 onion, chopped

5 garlic cloves, chopped

1 lb. ripe tomatoes

2 tortillas, preferably stale, cut into small pieces

pinch of cloves

pinch of fennel seeds

$1/8$ tsp. each ground cinnamon, coriander, and cumin

3 tbsp. lightly toasted sesame seeds or tahini

3 tbsp. flaked or coarsely ground blanched almonds

2 tbsp. raisins

1 tbsp. peanut butter (optional)

2 cups chicken stock

3-4 tbsp. grated unsweetened chocolate

2 tbsp. mild chili powder

3 tbsp. vegetable oil

about 1 tbsp. lime juice

salt and black pepper

1 Using metal tongs, toast each chili over an open flame for a few seconds until the color darkens. Alternatively, roast in an ungreased frying pan over a medium heat, turning constantly, for about 30 seconds.

2 Place the toasted chilies in a bowl or a pan and pour boiling water over to cover. Cover with a lid and leave to soften for

at least one hour or overnight. Once or twice lift the lid and rearrange the chilies so that they soak evenly.

3 Remove the softened chilies with a slotted spoon. Discard the stems and seeds and cut the flesh into pieces. Place in a blender.

4 Add the onion, garlic, tomatoes, tortillas, cloves,

fennel seeds, cinnamon, coriander, cumin, sesame seeds, almonds, raisins, and peanut butter if using, then process to combine. With the motor running, add enough stock through the feed tube to make a smooth paste. Stir in the remaining stock, chocolate, and chili powder.

5 Heat the oil in a heavy-based pan until it is smoking, then pour in the mole mixture. It will sputter and pop as it hits the hot oil. Cook for about 10 minutes, stirring occasionally to prevent it from burning. Season with salt, pepper, and lime juice, and serve.

Mole Verde

Moles are purées and, depending on the ingredients, they vary in color from yellow and green to chocolate brown. This green mole is a speciality of Jalisco. Serve with either warm corn tortillas or unfilled tamales.

Serves 4-6

INGREDIENTS

2 cups toasted pumpkin seeds

4 cups chicken stock

several pinches of ground cloves

8-10 tomatillos, diced or use 1 cup
  mild tomatillo salsa

½ onion, chopped

½ fresh green chili, deseeded and

diced

3 garlic cloves, chopped

½ tsp. fresh thyme leaves

½ tsp. fresh marjoram leaves

3 tbsp. lard or vegetable oil

3 bay leaves

4 tbsp. chopped fresh cilantro

salt and pepper

fresh green chili slices, to garnish

1 Grind the toasted pumpkin seeds in a food processor. Add half the chicken stock, the cloves, tomatillos, onion, chili, garlic, thyme, and marjoram and blend to a purée.

2 Heat the lard or oil in a heavy-based frying pan and add the puréed pumpkin seed mixture and the bay leaves. Cook over a medium-high heat for about 5 minutes until the mixture has thickened.

3 Remove from the heat and add the rest of the stock and the cilantro. Cook until it thickens, then remove from the heat. Remove the bay leaves and process until smooth again. Add salt and pepper to taste.

4 Transfer to a bowl, garnish with chili and serve.

VARIATIONS

Make a tamale dough (see page 138) and poach in the mole as dumplings making a filling snack.

Salsa, Tortillas, & Beans & Rice

Salsas appear on every table of every corner of Mexico, raw, cooked, chopped, chunky, smooth, spicy, mild, or fiery. They are what adds interest to often simple fare. What's more, they are delicious and good for you too, as long as you don't burn your tongue, that is! In this recipe you'll find the full range from sizzling Salsa Verde to powerful and smoky Chipotle Salsa and cooling Fresh Pineapple Salsa.

Tortillas are not only the bread of Mexico, they are also its knives and fork: break off a piece of tortilla, wrap it up in whatever you are eating, and you have an instant taco, no eating utensils needed. The variety of dishes made with tortillas in this chapter, range from fish-filled tacos and tostadas topped with chicken and green salsa, to burritos filled with lamb and black beans.

In Mexico, beans and rice are eaten every day, for nearly every meal: a pot of beans is almost always simmering on the back of nearly every stove in the land, and great pots of rice are cooked using the stock of simmering meats for soups and other dishes. Discover how the make the famous Mexican refried beans, and learn the secret of Green Rice—a delicious dish, flavored with roasted onions, garlic, chili, and plenty of cilantro.

If you ate nothing but salsas, dishes of tortillas, beans and rice, you would be eating the very soul of Mexico.

Classic Salsas

A Mexican meal is not complete without an accompanying salsa. These two traditional salsas are ideal for seasoning any dish, from filled tortillas to broiled meat—they add a spicy hotness that is the very essence of Mexican cooking.

Serves 4-6

INGREDIENTS

JALAPEÑO SALSA

1 onion, finely chopped

2-3 garlic cloves, finely chopped

4-6 tbsp. coarsely chopped pickled jalapeños

juice of ½ lemon

about ¼ tsp. ground cumin

salt

SALSA CRUDA:

6-8 ripe tomatoes, finely chopped

scant ½ cup tomato juice

3-4 garlic cloves, finely chopped

½-1 bunch fresh cilantro leaves, coarsely chopped

pinch of sugar

3-4 fresh green chilies, such as

jalapeño or serrano, deseeded and finely chopped

½-1 tsp. ground cumin

3-4 scallions, finely chopped

salt

1 To make the jalapeño salsa, put the onion in a bowl with the garlic, jalapeños, lemon juice, and cumin. Season with salt and stir together. Cover and chill until required.

2 To make a chunky-textured salsa cruda, stir all the ingredients together in a bowl, adding salt to taste. Cover and chill until required.

3 To make a smooth-textured salsa, put all the ingredients in a blender or food processor and process until well blended. Cover

VARIATIONS

For the salsa cruda, substitute finely chopped orange segments and deseeded diced cucumber for the tomatoes to add a fresh fruity taste.

and chill until required.

COOK'S TIP

You can vary the amount of garlic, chillies and ground spices according to taste, but make sure the salsa has quite a 'kick', otherwise it will not be effective.

Chipotle Salsa

Chipotles are the smoked jalapeño chili sold either dried or in cans, packed in a spicy flavorful marinade called "adobo." Here the marinade from the canned version is used to perk up a simple fresh tomato salsa.

Makes about 2 cups

INGREDIENTS

1 lb. ripe juicy tomatoes, diced
3–5 garlic cloves, finely chopped
½ bunch fresh cilantro leaves, coarsely chopped
1 small onion, chopped

1–2 tsp. adobo marinade from canned chipotle chilies
½–1 tsp. sugar
lime juice, to taste
salt

pinch of cinnamon (optional)
pinch of ground allspice (optional)
pinch of ground cumin (optional)

1 Put the tomatoes, garlic, and cilantro in a blender or food processor.

2 Process the mixture until it is smooth, then add the onion, adobo marinade, sugar, lime juice, and salt to taste. Add the cinnamon, allspice, or cumin, if desired.

3 Serve at once, or cover and chill until ready to serve, although the salsa is at its best when served freshly made.

COOK'S TIP

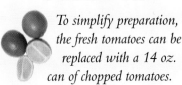

To simplify preparation, the fresh tomatoes can be replaced with a 14 oz. can of chopped tomatoes.

COOK'S TIP

Canned chipotle chillies are available from specialist Mexican stores.

Cooked Chipotle Salsa

This rich, tomato-red chipotle salsa is sweet and tangy, delicious with anything barbecued, or dabbed into a taco or burrito.

Makes about 2 cups

INGREDIENTS

3 dried chipotle chilies
1 onion, finely chopped
14 oz. can tomatoes, including their
   juices
2-3 tbsp. dark brown sugar

2-3 garlic cloves, finely chopped
pinch of ground cinnamon
pinch of ground cloves or allspice
large pinch of ground cumin
juice of ½ lemon

1 tbsp. extra-virgin olive oil
lemon rind strips, to garnish

1 Place the chilies in a pan with enough water to cover. Protecting your face against fumes and making sure the kitchen is well ventilated, bring the chilies and water to a boil. Cook for about 5 minutes, then remove from heat, cover and leave to stand until softened.

2 Remove the chilies from the water with a slotted spoon. Cut away and discard the stem and seeds, then either scrape the flesh from the skins or chop up the whole chilies.

3 Put the onions in a pan with the tomatoes and sugar and cook over a medium heat, stirring, until thickened.

4 Remove from the heat and add the garlic, cinnamon, cloves, cumin, lemon juice, olive oil, and prepared chipotle chilies. Season with salt to taste and leave to cool. Serve garnished with lemon rind.

COOK'S TIP

Do not inhale the fumes given off by the boiling chilies as they can irritate your lungs.

COOK'S TIP

This salsa freezes extremely well. Freeze in an ice-cube tray, then pop the cubes out and store in a plastic bag, ready to use for individual portions.

Hot Mexican Salsas

These salsas capture the inimitable tangy, spicy flavor of Mexico. Choose from a fresh minty fruit salsa, a spicy "green" salsa, or a charred chili salsa to give a touch of hotness to any Mexican meal.

Serves 4–6

INGREDIENTS

TROPICAL FRUIT SALSA:
½ sweet ripe pineapple, peeled, cored and diced
1 mango or papaya, peeled, deseeded and diced
½–1 fresh green chili, such as jalapeño or serrano, deseeded and chopped
½–1 fresh red chili, such as jalapeño or serrano, chopped
½ red onion, chopped
1 tbsp. sugar
juice of 1 lime
3 tbsp. chopped fresh mint
salt

SCORCHED CHILI SALSA:
1 green bell pepper
2-3 fresh green chilies, such as jalapeño or serrano
2 garlic cloves, finely chopped
juice of ½ lime
1 tsp. salt
large pinch of dried oregano
large pinch of ground cumin
2-3 tbsp. extra-virgin olive oil or vegetable oil

SALSA VERDE:
1 lb. oz. fresh tomatillos, husks removed, cooked in a small amount of water until just tender, then chopped
1-2 fresh green chilies, such as jalapeño or serrano, deseeded and finely chopped
1 green bell pepper or large mild green chili, such as Anaheim or poblano, deseeded and chopped
1 small onion, chopped
1 bunch fresh cilantro leaves, finely chopped
½ tsp. ground cumin
salt

1 To make the tropical fruit salsa, combine all the ingredients in a large bowl, adding salt to taste. Cover the bowl and chill in the refrigerator until required.

2 For scorched chili salsa, char the chilies and bell pepper in an ungreased frying pan. Cool, deseed, skin and chop. Mix with the garlic, lime juice, salt, and oil. Top with oregano and cumin.

3 For salsa verde, combine the ingredients in a bowl, adding salt to taste. If a smoother sauce is preferred, blend the ingredients in a food processor. Spoon into a bowl to serve.

Salsa of Marinated Chipotle Chilies

Dried chipotle chilies make a spicy-sweet smoky relish, good for adding to tostadas, tacos, and any other tortilla dish.

Makes about 2½ cups

INGREDIENTS

6 dried chipotle chilies
6 tbsp. tomato ketchup
12 oz. ripe tomatoes, diced
1 large onion, chopped
5 garlic cloves, chopped
2 tbsp. cider vinegar
1¼ cups water

1 tbsp. extra-virgin olive oil
2 tbsp. sugar, preferably molasses sugar
pinch of salt
¼ tsp. ground allspice
¼ tsp. ground cloves
¼ tsp. ground cinnamon

¼ tsp. ground cumin
3-4 tbsp. lime juice or combination of pineapple and lemon juice
pepper

1 Place the chipotles in a pan with enough water to cover. Bring to a boil, taking care not to inhale the fumes given off as they can irritate your lungs. Simmer, covered, for about 20 minutes, then remove from the heat and leave to cool.

2 Remove the chilies from the water. Cut away and discard the stem and seeds, then either scrape the flesh from the skins or chop up the whole chilies.

3 Place the ketchup and tomatoes in a pan with the onion, chilies, garlic, vinegar, water, olive oil, sugar, salt, allspice, cloves, cinnamon, and cumin. Bring to a boil. Reduce the heat and simmer for about 15 minutes until the mixture has thickened.

4 Season with salt and pepper to taste, then stir in the fruit juice and use as required.

Fresh Pineapple Salsa

This sweet fruity salsa is fresh and fragrant, a wonderful foil to spicy food from the barbecue.

Serves 4

INGREDIENTS

½ ripe pineapple
juice of 1 lime or lemon
1 garlic clove, finely chopped
1 scallion, thinly sliced

½–1 fresh green or red chili, deseeded
and finely chopped
½ red bell pepper, deseeded and
chopped

3 tbsp. chopped fresh mint
3 tbsp. chopped fresh cilantro
pinch of salt

1 Using a sharp knife, cut off the top and bottom of the pineapple. Place upright on a board, then slice off the skin, cutting downward. Cut the flesh into slices, halve the slices, and remove the cores, if desired. Dice the flesh. Reserve any juice that accumulates as you cut the pineapple.

2 Place the pineapple in a bowl and stir in the lime juice, garlic, scallion, chopped chili, and red bell pepper.

3 Stir in the chopped fresh mint and cilantro. Add the salt and sugar and stir well to combine all the ingredients. Chill until ready to serve.

COOK'S TIP

A fresh pineapple is ripe if it has a sweet aroma. The flesh will still be fairly firm to touch. Still, fresh-looking leaves are a sign of good condition.

VARIATION

Replace the pineapple with 3 juicy oranges, peeled and divided into segments.

Crab & Avocado
Soft Tacos

Crab meat and avocado make an elegant yet very authentic filling for tacos.
Eat one and you will be transported to a beach somewhere south of Acapulco!

Serves 4

INGREDIENTS

8 soft corn tortillas
1 avocado
lime or lemon juice, for tossing
4-6 tbsp. sour cream
9-10 oz. cooked crab meat
½ lime

½ fresh green chili, such as jalapeño
 or serrano, deseeded and chopped
 or thinly sliced
1 ripe tomato, deseeded and diced
½ small onion, finely chopped
2 tbsp. chopped fresh cilantro

salsa of your choice, to serve
(optional)

1 Heat the tortillas in an ungreased nonstick frying pan in a stack, alternating the top and bottom tortillas so that they heat evenly. Wrap in aluminum foil or a clean dishtowel to keep warm.

2 Cut the avocado in half around the pit. Twist apart, then remove the pit with a knife. Carefully peel off the skin, slice the flesh and toss in lime or lemon juice to prevent discoloration.

3 Spread one tortilla with sour cream. Top with crab meat, a squeeze of lime, and a sprinkling of chili, tomato, onion, cilantro and avocado, adding a splash of salsa if desired. Repeat with the remaining tortillas and serve at once.

VARIATIONS

To transform into tostadas, fry the tortillas in a small amount of oil in a nonstick pan until crisp. Top one crisp tortilla with the filling, as in Step 3. Prepare a second tortilla with the filling and place on top of the first filled tortilla. Repeat once more, to make a small tower, top with shredded lettuce and serve.

Fish Tacos Ensenada Style

These tacos of fried fish chunks and red cabbage salad are served up in the cantinas and fondas of the coastal town of Ensenada, in Mexico's Baja California.

Serves 4

INGREDIENTS

1 lb. firm-fleshed white fish, such as
    red snapper or cod
¼ tsp. dried oregano
¼ tsp. ground cumin
1 tsp. mild chili powder
2–3 garlic cloves, finely chopped

3 tbsp. all-purpose flour
vegetable oil, for frying
¼ red cabbage, thinly sliced or
    shredded
juice of 2 limes
hot pepper sauce or salsa to taste

8 soft corn tortillas
1 tbsp. chopped fresh cilantro
½ onion, chopped (optional)
salt and pepper
salsa of your choice

1 Place the fish on a plate and sprinkle with half the oregano, cumin, chili powder, garlic, and salt and pepper, then dust with the flour.

2 Heat the oil in a frying pan until it is smoking, then fry the fish in several batches until it is golden on the outside, and just tender in the middle. Remove from the pan and place on paper towels to drain.

3 Combine the cabbage with the remaining oregano, cumin, chili, and garlic, then stir in the lime juice, and salt and hot pepper sauce to taste. Set aside.

4 Heat the tortillas in an ungreased nonstick frying pan, sprinkling with a few drops of water as they heat; wrap the tortillas in a clean dishtowel as you work to keep them warm. Alternatively, heat through in a

stack in the pan, alternating the top and bottom tortillas so that they warm evenly.

5 Place some of the warm fried fish in each tortilla, along with a big spoonful of the cabbage salad. Sprinkle with fresh cilantro and onion, if using. Add salsa to taste and serve at once.

Fish & Refried Bean Tostadas with Green Salsa

Crisp tostadas are topped with spiced fish, refried beans, and crunchy lettuce— perfect for a well-balanced lunch.

Serves 4

INGREDIENTS

1 lb. firm-fleshed white fish, such as red snapper or cod

½ cup fish stock, or water mixed with a fish stock cube

¼ tsp. ground cumin

¼ tsp. mild chili powder

pinch of dried oregano

4 garlic cloves, finely chopped

juice of ½ lemon or lime

8 soft corn tortillas

vegetable oil, for frying

14 oz. can refried beans, warmed with 2 tbsp. water to thin

½ quantity Salsa Verde (see page 102)

2-3 leaves romaine lettuce, shredded

3 tbsp. chopped fresh fresh cilantro

2 tbsp. chopped onion

salt and pepper

TO GARNISH:

sour cream

chopped fresh herbs

1 Put the fish in a pan with the fish stock, cumin, chili, oregano, garlic, and salt and pepper. Gently bring to a boil, then immediately remove from the heat and leave the fish to cool in the cooking liquid.

2 When cool enough to handle, remove from the liquid with a slotted spoon; reserve the cooking liquid. Break the fish up into bites-sized pieces, put in a bowl, sprinkle with the lemon or lime juice and set aside.

3 To make tostadas, fry the tortillas in a small amount of oil in a nonstick pan until crisp. Spread the tostadas with the warm refried beans.

4 Gently reheat the fish with a little of the reserved cooking liquid, then spoon it on top of the beans. Top each tostada with some of the salsa, lettuce, fresh cilantro, and onion. Garnish each with a dollop of sour cream and a sprinkling of cilantro. Serve immediately.

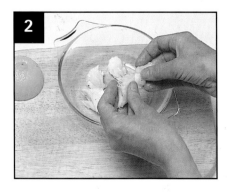

Fish Soft Tacos

You can use any seafood you like in this tasty Mexican snack.
Tacos are eaten in the hand, like sandwiches.

Serves 4-6

INGREDIENTS

1 lb. firm-fleshed white fish, such as
   red snapper or cod
¼ tsp. ground cumin
pinch of dried oregano
4 garlic finely cloves, chopped

½ cup fish stock, or water mixed with
   a fish stock cube
juice of ½ lemon or lime
8 soft corn tortillas
2 ripe tomatoes, diced

1 quantity Salsa Cruda (see page 96)
2-3 leaves romaine lettuce, shredded
salt and pepper
lemon slices, to serve

1 Season the fish with salt and pepper, then put in a pan with the cumin, oregano, garlic, and enough fish stock to cover.

2 Bring to a boil, then cook for about a minute. Remove the pan from the heat and leave the fish to cool in the cooking liquid for about 30 minutes.

3 Remove the fish from the stock and break up into bite sized pieces. Sprinkle with the lemon or lime juice and set aside.

4 Heat the tortillas in an ungreased nonstick frying pan, sprinkling them with a few drops of water as they heat; wrap in a clean dishtowel as you work to keep them warm. Alternatively, heat through in a stack in the pan, alternating the top and bottom tortillas so that they warm evenly.

5 Arrange shredded lettuce in the middle of one tortilla, spoon on a few big chunks of the fish, then sprinkle with the tomato. Add salsa cruda. Repeat with the

remaining tortillas and serve immediately with lemon slices.

VARIATIONS

Cook several peeled waxy potatoes in the fish stock, then dice and serve wrapped up in the warm tortillas along with the lettuce, fish, tomato, and salsa. Or add sliced lime-dressed avocado with the filling.

Chicken Tacos from Puebla

Seasoned chicken fills these soft tacos, along with creamy refried beans, avocado, smoky chipotle, and sour cream. A feast of tastes!

Serves 4

INGREDIENTS

8-12 oz. leftover cooked chicken, diced or shredded

2 tsp. vegetable oil

8 soft corn tortillas

8 oz. can refried beans, warmed with a 2 tbsp. water to thin

¼ tsp. ground cumin

¼ tsp. dried oregano

1 avocado, pitted, sliced and tossed with lime juice

Salsa Verde (see page 102) or salsa of your choice

1 canned chipotle chili in adobo marinade, chopped, or bottled

chipotle salsa

¾ cup sour cream

½ onion, chopped

handful of lettuce leaves

5 radishes, diced

salt and pepper

1 Heat the tortillas in an ungreased nonstick frying pan in a stack, alternating the top and bottom tortillas so that the tortillas heat evenly. Wrap in aluminum foil or a clean dishtowel to keep warm.

2 Heat the oil in a frying pan, add the chicken and heat through. Season with salt and pepper to taste.

3 Combine the refried beans with the cumin and oregano.

4 Spread one tortilla with warm refried beans, then top with a spoonful of the chicken, a slice or two of avocado, a dab of salsa, chipotle to taste, a dollop of sour cream, and a sprinkling of onion, lettuce, and radishes. Season with salt and pepper to taste, then roll up, as tightly as you can. Repeat with the remaining tortillas and serve at once.

VARIATIONS

Replace the chicken with 1 lb. ground beef browned with a seasoning of chopped onion, mild chili powder, and ground cumin to taste.

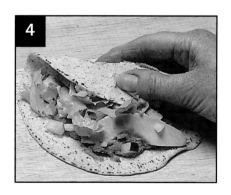

Chile Verde Tacos with Pinto Beans

*This is also an ideal way of using up any leftover spicy stewed meat—
use in place of the chile verde and you have an almost instant meal!*

Serves 4

INGREDIENTS

8 soft corn tortillas
vegetable oil, for greasing
14 oz. can pinto beans
¹⁄₃ quantity Chile Verde
  (see page 204)
3 ripe tomatoes, diced

½ onion, chopped
2 tbsp. finely chopped fresh
  cilantro

TO GARNISH:
sour cream

mild chili powder

TO SERVE:
salsa of your choice
shredded lettuce

1 Heat the tortillas in a lightly greased nonstick frying pan; wrap the tortillas in aluminum foil or a dishtowel as you work to keep them warm.

2 Drain the beans, reserving a few tablespoons of the liquid. Heat the beans in a pan with the reserved canned liquid.

3 Heat through the chile verde in another pan.

4 Spoon some of the drained beans on to a warm tortilla. Top with warm chile verde, then sprinkle with tomatoes, onion, and fresh cilantro. Roll up and repeat with the remaining tortillas. Garnish with a spoonful of sour cream and a sprinkling of chili powder, then serve at once with salsa and shredded lettuce.

VARIATIONS

For a tostada version, heat tostadas (crisp tortillas) under the broiler, then spread with warmed slightly thinned refried beans and top with the chile verde, shredded lettuce, a little grated pecorino cheese, salsa, onion, fresh cilantro, and sour cream. Serve at once.

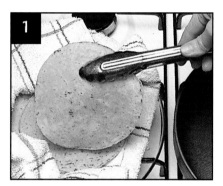

Chicken Tostadas with Green Salsa & Chipotle

Chicken makes a delicate yet satisfying topping for crisp tostadas. You do not need to prepare chicken especially for this recipe: any leftover chicken is equally delicious.

Serves 4–6

INGREDIENTS

6 soft corn tortillas

vegetable oil, for frying

1 lb. skinned boned chicken breast or thigh, cut into strips or small pieces

1 cup chicken stock

2 garlic cloves, finely chopped

1 tbsp. chopped fresh cilantro

14 oz. refried beans (see page 144) or canned

large pinch of ground cumin

8 oz. grated cheese

2 ripe tomatoes, diced

handful of crisp lettuce leaves, such as romaine or iceberg, shredded

4–6 radishes, diced

3 scallions, thinly sliced

1 ripe avocado, pitted, diced or sliced and tossed with lime juice

1–2 canned chipotle chilies in adobo marinade, or dried chipotle reconstituted (see page 100), cut into thin strips

1 To make tostadas, fry the tortillas in a small amount of oil in a nonstick pan until crisp.

2 Put the chicken in a pan with the stock and garlic. Bring to a boil, then reduce the heat and cook for 1–2 minutes until the chicken begins to turn opaque.

3 Remove the chicken from the heat and leave to steep in its hot liquid to cook through.

4 Heat the beans with enough water to form a smooth purée. Add the cumin and keep warm.

5 Reheat the tostadas under a preheated broiler, if necessary.

Spread the hot beans on the tostadas, then sprinkle with the grated cheese. Lift the cooked chicken from the liquid and divide between the tostadas. Sprinkle with the cilantro and top with the tomatoes, lettuce, radishes, scallions, avocado, sour cream, and a few strips of chipotle. Serve immediately.

Vegetable Tostadas

*Top a crisp tostada (fried tortilla) with spicy vegetables
and you have a vegetarian feast!*

Serves 4

INGREDIENTS

4 soft corn tortillas

vegetable oil, for frying

2 potatoes, diced

1 carrot, diced

2-3 tbsp. extra-virgin olive oil or
   vegetable oil

3 garlic cloves, finely chopped

1 red bell pepper, deseeded and diced

1 tsp. mild chili powder

1 tsp. paprika

½ tsp. ground cumin

3-4 ripe tomatoes, diced

4 oz. green beans, blanched and cut
   into bite-sized lengths

several large pinches dried oregano

14 oz. cooked black beans, drained

8 oz. crumbled feta cheese

3-4 leaves romaine lettuce, shredded

3-4 scallions, thinly sliced

salt and pepper

1 To make tostadas, fry the tortillas in a small amount of oil in a nonstick pan until crisp.

2 Heat the olive oil in a frying pan, add the potatoes and carrot and cook until softened. Add the garlic, red bell pepper, chili powder, paprika, and cumin. Cook for 2-3 minutes until the peppers have softened.

3 Add the tomatoes, green beans and oregano. Cook for 8-10 minutes until the vegetables are tender and form a sauce-like mixture. The mixture should not be too dry; add a little water if necessary, to keep it moist.

4 Heat the black beans in a pan with a tiny amount of water, and keep warm. Reheat the tostadas under the broiler.

5 Layer the beans over the hot tostadas, then sprinkle with the cheese and top with a few spoonfuls of the hot vegetables in sauce. Serve at once, each tostada sprinkled with the lettuce and scallions.

Broccoli Enchiladas in Mild Chili Salsa

This is reminiscent of a sort of Mexican spiced cannelloni, with flour tortillas taking the place of the pasta tubes.

Serves 4

INGREDIENTS

1 lb. broccoli florets
8 oz. ricotta cheese
1 garlic clove, chopped
½ tsp. ground cumin
6-8 oz. cheddar cheese, grated
6-8 tbsp. freshly grated Parmesan
 cheese

1 egg, lightly beaten
4-6 flour tortillas
vegetable oil, for greasing
1 quantity Mild Red Chili Sauce
 (see page 86)
1 cup chicken or vegetable stock
½ onion, finely chopped

3-4 tbsp. chopped fresh cilantro
3 ripe tomatoes, diced
salt and pepper
hot salsa (see page 102), to serve

1 Bring a pan of salted water to a boil, add the broccoli, bring back to a boil and blanch for 1 minute. Drain, refresh under cold running water, then drain again. Cut off the stems, peel, and chop. Dice the broccoli heads.

2 Mix the broccoli with the ricotta cheese, garlic, cumin, half the cheddar and half the Parmesan in a bowl. Mix in the egg and season.

3 Heat the tortillas in a lightly greased nonstick frying pan; wrap the tortillas in aluminum foil. Fill the tortillas with the broccoli mixture, rolling them up.

4 Arrange the tortilla rolls in an ovenproof dish, large enough to hold them in a single layer, then pour the mild chili sauce over the top. Pour over the stock.

5 Top with the remaining cheddar and Parmesan cheeses and bake in a preheated oven at 375° F for about 30 minutes. Serve sprinkled with the onion, fresh cilantro, and tomatoes. Serve with a hot salsa.

Cheese Enchiladas with Mole Flavors

Mole sauce makes a delicious enchilada—a good reason to make yourself a big pot of Mole Poblano (see page 90). But if you are short of time, you can always use bottled mole paste instead.

Serves 4-6

INGREDIENTS

8 soft corn tortillas
vegetable oil, for greasing
2 cups mole sauce
1 cup chicken or vegetable stock
8 oz. grated cheese, such as cheddar,
   mozzarella, asiago, or Mexican

queso oaxaco, one type or a
  mixture
5 scallions, thinly sliced
2-3 tbsp. chopped fresh cilantro
handful of romaine lettuce leaves,
  shredded

1 avocado, pitted, diced, and tossed in
  lime juice
6-8 tbsp. sour cream
salsa of your choice

1 Heat the tortillas in a lightly greased nonstick frying pan; wrap the tortillas in aluminum foil as you work to keep them warm.

2 Dip the tortillas into the mole sauce, and pile up on a plate. Fill the inside of the top sauced tortilla with a few spoonfuls of cheese. Roll up and arrange in a shallow ovenproof dish. Repeat this process with the remaining

tortillas, reserving a handful of the cheese to sprinkle over the top

3 Pour the rest of the mole sauce over the rolled tortillas, then pour the stock over the top. Sprinkle with the reserved cheese and cover with aluminum foil.

4 Bake in a preheated oven at 375° F until the cheese filling melts, about 20 minutes.

5 Arrange the scallions, fresh cilantro, lettuce, avocado and sour cream on top. Add salsa to taste. Serve at once.

Santa Fe
Red Chili Enchiladas

These enchiladas are served stacked, in the traditional New Mexican style,
but you can always roll them up with the filling if you prefer.

Serves 4-6

INGREDIENTS

4 cups vegetable, chicken or beef
   stock, simmering
2-3 tbsp. masa harina or 1 corn
   tortilla, crushed or crumbled
4 tbsp. mild chili powder, such as New
   Mexico
2 tbsp. paprika
2 garlic cloves, finely chopped
¼ tsp. ground cumin

pinch of ground cinnamon
pinch of ground allspice
pinch of dried oregano
1 tbsp. lime juice
1-2 tbsp. extra-virgin olive oil
12 flour tortillas
about 1 lb. cooked chicken or pork,
   cut into pieces

3 oz. grated cheese
4-6 eggs

TO SERVE:
½ onion, finely chopped
1 tbsp. finely chopped fresh cilantro
salsa of your choice

1 Mix the masa harina with the chili powder, paprika, garlic, cumin, cinnamon, allspice, oregano, and enough water to make a thin paste. Process in a blender or food processor until smooth.

2 Stir the paste into the simmering stock, reduce the heat and cook until it thickens slightly, then remove the sauce from the heat and stir in the lime juice.

3 Dip the tortillas into the warm sauce. Cover one tortilla with some filling. Top with a second dipped tortilla and more filling. Make 1-2 more towers in this way, then transfer to an ovenproof dish.

4 Pour the remaining sauce over the tortillas, then sprinkle with the grated cheese. Bake in a preheated oven at 350° F for 15-20 minutes or until the cheese has melted.

5 Meanwhile, heat the olive oil in a nonstick frying pan and cook the eggs until the whites are set and the yolks are still soft.

6 Serve cut into wedges and topped with an egg. Serve with the onion, cilantro, and salsa.

Chicken Tortilla Flutes with Guacamole

These crisply fried, rolled tortillas are known as flauta, meaning "flutes" in Mexican because of their delicate, long shape.

Serves 4

INGREDIENTS

12 oz. cooked chicken, diced
1 tsp. mild chili powder
1 onion, chopped
2 tbsp. finely chopped fresh cilantro
1-2 tbsp. crème fraîche

8 soft corn tortillas
vegetable oil, for frying
1 quantity of Guacamole
  (see page 28)
salsa of your choice

3-4 ripe tomatoes, diced
salt

1 Heat the tortillas in an ungreased nonstick frying pan in a stack, alternating the top and bottom tortillas so that all of the tortillas warm evenly. Wrap in aluminum foil or a clean dishtowel to keep warm.

2 Place the chicken in a bowl with the chili powder, half the onion, half the cilantro and salt to taste. Add enough crème fraîche to hold the mixture together.

3 Arrange 2 corn tortillas on the work surface so that they are overlapping, then spoon some of the filling along the center. Roll up very tightly and secure in place roll with a toothpick or two. Repeat with the remaining tortillas and filling.

4 Heat oil in a deep frying pan until hot and fry the rolls until golden and crisp. Drain on paper towels.

5 Serve immediately, garnishing with the guacamole, salsa, diced tomato and the remaining onion and fresh cilantro.

VARIATIONS

Replace the chicken with seafood, such as cooked shrimp or crab meat, and serve with lemon wedges.

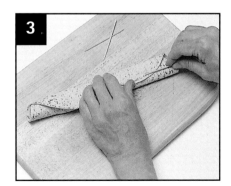

Pork Quesadilla with Pinto Beans

These melt-in-the-mouth tortilla parcels have a lovely pork, beans, and melted cheese filling.
Any leftover cooked meat may be used instead of the Carnitas.

Serves 4

INGREDIENTS

1 quantity of Carnitas (see page 208) or about 3½ oz. cooked pork strips per person
1 ripe tomato, deseeded and diced
½ onion, chopped
3 tbsp. chopped fresh cilantro
4 large flour tortillas
12 oz. grated or thinly sliced cheese,

such as mozzarella or gouda
about 13½ oz. cooked drained pinto beans
hot salsa (see page 102) or bottled hot sauce, to taste
pickled jalapeño chilies, cut into thin rings, to taste
vegetable oil, for frying

TO SERVE:
pickled chilies
mixed salad

1 Heat the carnitas in a pan and keep hot over a low heat.

2 Combine the tomato, onion, and cilantro in a bowl and set aside.

3 Heat a tortilla in an ungreased nonstick frying pan. Sprinkle the tortilla with cheese, then top with some of the meat, beans, and reserved tomato mixture. Add salsa and pickled jalapeños to taste. Fold over the sides to make a parcel. Repeat this process with the remaining tortillas.

4 Heat the parcels gently on each side in the frying pan, adding a few drops of oil to keep it all supple and succulent, until the tortilla is golden and the cheese inside has melted. Keep warm. Repeat with the remaining tortillas and filling.

5 Transfer the quesadillas to a plate and serve at once, with pickled chilies and salad.

Casserole of Tortilla Chips & Chorizo

*Called chilaquiles in Mexican, this dish turns everyday leftovers into something quite special!
Excellent served for brunch, accompanied by an egg.*

Serves 6-8

INGREDIENTS

12 stale tortillas, cut into strips
1 tbsp. vegetable oil
2-3 chorizo sausages, thinly sliced or diced

2 garlic cloves, finely chopped
8 oz. chopped canned tomatoes
3 tbsp. chopped fresh cilantro
2 cups chicken or vegetable stock

8 oz. grated cheese
1 onion, finely chopped
salt and pepper

1 Place the tortilla strips in a roasting pan, toss with the oil and bake in a preheated oven at 375° F for about 30 minutes until they are crisp and golden.

2 Brown the chorizo with the garlic in a frying pan until the meat is cooked; pour away any excess fat. Add the tomatoes and the cilantro and season with salt and pepper to taste. Set aside.

3 In an ovenproof dish, about 12 inches square, layer the tortilla chips and chorizo mixture, finishing with the tortilla chips.

4 Pour the stock over the top of the dish, then sprinkle with the cheese. Bake in a preheated oven at 375° F for about 40 minutes until the cheese has melted and the tortilla chips are fairly soft.

5 Serve immediately, sprinkled with the chopped onion.

VARIATIONS

Serve with a fried egg or two alongside. The soft yolk tastes wonderful with the spicy casserole—offer a bowl of spicy salsa for those who want it hotter.

Green Chili & Chicken Chilaquiles

Easy to put together, this dish makes a perfect midweek supper.
Use tortilla chips instead of baking the tortillas, if you prefer.

Serves 4-6

INGREDIENTS

12 stale tortillas, cut into strips
1 tbsp. vegetable oil
1 small cooked chicken, meat removed from the bones and cut into bite-sized pieces
Salsa Verde (see page 102)
8 tbsp. chopped fresh cilantro
1 tsp. finely chopped fresh oregano

or thyme
4 garlic cloves, finely chopped
¼ tsp. ground cumin
2 cups chicken stock
12 oz. grated cheese, such as cheddar, manchego, or mozzarella
about 1⅓ cups freshly grated Parmesan cheese

TO SERVE:
1½ cup crème fraîche or sour cream
3-5 scallions, thinly sliced
pickled chilies

1 Place the tortilla strips in a roasting pan, toss with the oil and bake in a preheated oven at 375° F for about 30 minutes until they are crisp and golden.

2 Arrange the chicken in a 9 x 13 inch casserole, then sprinkle with half the salsa verse, cilantro, oregano, garlic, cumin, and cheese. Repeat these layers and top with the tortilla strips.

3 Pour the stock over the top, then sprinkle with the remaining cheeses.

4 Bake in a preheated oven at 375° F for about 30 minutes or until the cheese is lightly golden in areas.

5 Garnish with the crème fraîche, scallions, and pickled chilies to taste. Serve at once.

VARIATIONS

For a vegetarian Mexicana filling, add diced sautéed tofu and corn kernels in place of the chicken.

Tamales

Traditional Mexican fare, tamales are large dumplings of corn flour, stuffed with a moist filling, then wrapped in either banana leaves or husks of corn. They make attractive party food.

Serves 4

INGREDIENTS

6 tbsp. lard or vegetable shortening
½ tsp. salt
pinch of sugar
pinch of ground cumin
8 oz. masa harina
½ tsp. baking powder
about 1 cup beef, chicken or

vegetable stock
4 oz. cooked corn, mixed with a little grated cheese and chopped green chili
8-10 corn husks or several banana leaves, cut into 12 in. squares

TO SERVE:
shredded lettuce
salsa of your choice

1 If using corn husks, soak in hot water to cover for at least 3 hours or overnight. If using banana leaves, warm them by placing over an open flame for just a few seconds, to make them pliable.

2 To make the tamale dough, beat the lard or shortening until fluffy, then beat in the salt, sugar, cumin, masa harina, and baking powder until the mixture resembles tiny crumbs.

3 Add the stock very gradually, in several batches, beating until mixture becomes fluffy and resembles whipped cream

4 Spread 1-2 tablespoons of the tamale mixture on either a soaked and drained corn husk or a piece of pliable heated banana leaf.

5 Fill with the flavored corn. Fold the sides of the husks or leaves over the filling to totally enclose. Wrap the parcels

individually in squares of aluminum foil, and arrange in a steamer.

6 Fill the bottom of the steamer with hot water, cover, and bring to a boil. Cook for about 40-60 minutes, taking care to top up the water in the bottom of the steamer. Remove from the heat and serve with shredded lettuce and salsa.

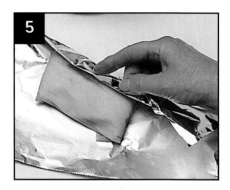

Burritos of Lamb & Black Beans

Stir-fried marinated lamb strips are paired with earthy black beans in these tasty burritos.

Serves 4

INGREDIENTS

1 lb. 5 oz. lean lamb
3 garlic cloves, finely chopped
juice of ½ lime
½ tsp. mild chili powder
½ tsp. ground cumin
large pinch of dried oregano leaves,

crushed
1-2 tbsp. extra-virgin olive oil
14 oz. cooked black beans, seasoned
  with a little cumin, salt and pepper
4 large flour tortillas
2-3 tbsp. chopped fresh cilantro

salsa, preferably Chipotle Salsa
  (see page 98)
salt and pepper

1 Slice the lamb into thin strips, then combine with the garlic, lime juice, chili powder, cumin, oregano, and olive oil. Season with salt and pepper. Marinate in the refrigerator for 4 hours.

2 Warm the black beans with a little water in a pan.

3 Heat the tortillas in an ungreased nonstick frying pan, sprinkling them with a few drops of water as they heat; wrap the tortillas in a clean dishtowel as you work to keep them warm. Alternatively, heat through in a stack in the pan, alternating the top and bottom tortillas so that they warm evenly. Wrap to keep warm.

4 Stir-fry the lamb in a heavy-based nonstick frying pan over high heat until browned on all sides. Remove from the heat.

5 Spoon some of the beans and browned meat into a tortilla, sprinkle with cilantro, then dab with salsa and roll up. Repeat with the remaining tortillas and serve at once.

VARIATIONS

Try adding a spoonful or two of cooked rice to each burrito.

Mexican Beans

A pot of beans, bubbling away on the stove, is the basic everyday food of Mexico—delicious and healthy!

Serves 4

INGREDIENTS

1 lb. 2 oz. dried pinto or cranberry
  beans
sprig of fresh mint
sprig of fresh thyme
sprig of fresh flat-leaf parsley

1 onion, cut into chunks
salt

TO SERVE:
shreds of scallion
warmed flour or corn tortillas

1 Pick through the beans and remove any bits of grit or stone. Cover the beans with cold water and leave to soak overnight. If you want to cut down on soaking time, bring the beans to a boil, cook for 5 minutes, then remove from the heat and leave to stand covered for 2 hours.

2 Drain the beans, place in a pan and cover with fresh water and the mint, thyme, and parsley. Bring to a boil, then reduce the heat to very low and cook gently, covered, for about 2 hours until

the beans are tender. The best way to check that they are done is to sample a bean or two every so often, after 1 3/4 hours cooking time.

3 Add the onion and continue to cook until the onion and beans are very tender.

4 To serve as a side dish, drain, season with salt and serve in a bowl lined with warmed corn or flour tortillas, garnished with scallion shreds (see Cook's Tip).

COOK'S TIP

If using the beans for Refried Beans (see page 144), do not drain as the liquid is required for the recipe.

COOK'S TIP

The length of time the beans take to cook will depend on the age of the beans—old beans take longer than younger beans; the mineral content of the water matters, too.

Refried Beans

One of Mexico's most famous dishes, refried beans, or frijoles refritos, are incredibly versatile.
Serve them piled on to crisp tostadas or crusty rolls, spooned beside rice or rolled into a tortilla.

Serves 4-6

INGREDIENTS

1 quantity Mexican Beans, with their cooking liquid (see page 142)
1-2 onions, chopped

½ cup vegetable oil or 4 ½ oz. lard or dripping
½ tsp. ground cumin

salt
9 oz. grated cheddar cheese (optional)

1 Put two-thirds of the cooked beans, with their cooking liquid, in a food processor and process to a purée. Stir in the remaining whole beans. Set aside.

2 Heat the oil or fat in a heavy-based frying pan. Add the onions and cook until they are very soft. Sprinkle with cumin and salt to taste.

3 Ladle in a cupful of the bean mixture, and cook, stirring, until the beans reduce down to a thick mixture; the beans will darken slightly as they cook.

4 Continue adding the bean mixture, a ladleful at a time, stirring and reducing down the liquid before adding the next ladleful. You should end up with a thick, chunky purée.

5 If using cheese, sprinkle it over the beans and cover tightly until the heat in the pan melts the cheese. Alternatively, place under a preheated broiler to melt the cheese. Serve immediately.

VARIATIONS

Add several browned, broken-up chorizo sausages to the beans, along with a small tin of sardines, mashed to a paste. Serve stuffed into crusty rolls for a classic mollete, or as a party dip. Good spread on to crisp tostadas for an afternoon snack.

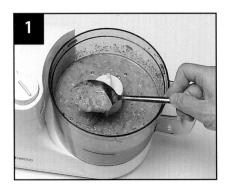

Mexican Refried Beans
"with everything"

These are refried beans fit for a fiesta, rich with everything: bacon, fried onions, tomatoes,
even a bit of beer! As delicious as it sounds!

Serves 4

INGREDIENTS

1-2 tbsp. vegetable oil

1-1½ large onions, chopped

4½ oz. bacon cut into small pieces

3-4 garlic cloves, finely chopped

about 1 tsp. ground cumin

½ tsp. mild chili powder

14 oz. can tomatoes, diced and

drained, reserving about $^2/_3$-$^3/_4$ cup
of their juices

14 oz. refried beans, broken up into
pieces

scant ½ cup beer

14 oz. can pinto beans, drained

salt and pepper

TO SERVE:

warmed flour tortillas

sour cream

sliced pickled chilies

1 Heat the oil in a frying pan. Add the onion and bacon and fry for about 5 minutes until they are just turning brown. Stir in the garlic, cumin, and chili powder and continue to cook for a minute. Add the tomatoes and cook over a medium-high heat until the liquid has evaporated.

2 Add the refried beans and mash lightly in the pan with the tomato mixture, adding beer as needed to thin out the beans and make them smoother. Lower the heat and cook, stirring, until the mixture is smooth and creamy.

3 Add the pinto beans and stir well to combine; if the mixture is too thick, add a little of the reserved tomato juice. Adjust the spicing to taste. Season with salt and pepper and serve with warmed tortillas, sour cream, and sliced chilies.

VARIATIONS

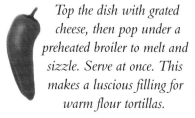

Top the dish with grated cheese, then pop under a preheated broiler to melt and sizzle. Serve at once. This makes a luscious filling for warm flour tortillas.

Spicy Fragrant Black Bean Chili

Black beans are fragrant and flavorful; enjoy this chilied bean stew Mexican style with soft tortillas, or Californian style, in a bowl with crisp tortillas chips crumbled in.

Serves 4

INGREDIENTS

14 oz. dried black beans
2 tbsp. olive oil
1 onion, chopped
5 garlic cloves, coarsely chopped
2 slices bacon, diced

½–1 tsp. ground cumin
½–1 tsp. mild red chili powder
1 red bell pepper, diced
1 carrot, diced
14 oz. fresh tomatoes, diced, or

chopped canned
1 bunch fresh cilantro, coarsely
chopped
salt and pepper

1 Soak the beans overnight, then drain. Put in a pan, cover with water and bring to a boil. Boil for 10 minutes, then reduce the heat and simmer for about 1½ hours until tender. Drain well, reserving 1 cup of the cooking liquid.

2 Heat the oil in a frying pan. Add the onion and garlic and fry for 2 minutes, stirring. Stir in the bacon, if using, and cook, stirring occasionally, until the bacon is cooked and the onions are softened.

3 Stir in the cumin and red chili powder and continue to cook for a moment or two. Add the red bell pepper, carrot and tomatoes. Cook over a medium heat for about 5 minutes.

4 Add half the cilantro and the beans and their reserved liquid. Season with salt and pepper. Simmer for 30-45 minutes or until very flavorful and thickened.

5 Stir through the remaining cilantro, adjust the seasoning and serve at once.

COOK'S TIP

You can use canned beans, if wished: drain and use 1 cup water for the liquid in Step 4.

Rice with Lime

The tangy citrus taste of lime is marvelous with all sorts of rice dishes, especially this typical Mexican rice, enriched with sautéed onions and garlic.

Serves 4

INGREDIENTS

6 oz. mixed long-grain and wild rice
2 tbsp. vegetable oil
1 small onion, finely chopped

3 garlic cloves, finely chopped
2 cups chicken or vegetable stock
juice of 1 lime

1 tbsp. chopped fresh cilantro

1 Heat the oil in a heavy-based pan or flameproof casserole. Add the onion and garlic and cook gently, stirring occasionally, for 2 minutes. Add the rice and cook for an additional minute, stirring. Pour in the stock, increase the heat and bring the rice to a boil. Reduce the heat to a very low simmer.

2 Cover and cook the rice for about 10 minutes or until the rice is just tender and the liquid is absorbed.

3 Sprinkle in the lime juice and fork the rice to fluff up and to mix the juice in. Sprinkle with the cilantro and serve.

COOK'S TIP

Garnish the rice with sautéed plantains: slice a ripe peeled plantain, preferably on the diagonal, then fry in a heavy-based pan in a small amount of oil until they have browned in spots and are tender. Arrange in the bowl of rice.

VARIATIONS

Fork about 8 oz. cooked corn into the rice when it is almost but not quite cooked, then allow the corn to warm through as the rice finishes cooking. Sprinkle with diced cucumber and a squeeze of lime juice to add a fresh tang.

Cumin Rice
with Sweet Bell Peppers

Cumin seeds add a distinctive flavor to this colorful rice dish.
Serve as a side dish for any roasted or barbecued meat.

Serves 4

INGREDIENTS

2 tbsp. butter

1 tbsp. vegetable oil

1 green bell pepper, deseeded
  and sliced

1 red bell pepper, deseeded

and sliced

3 scallions,
  thinly sliced

3-4 garlic cloves, finely chopped

6 oz. long-grain rice

1½ tsp. cumin seeds

½ tsp. dried oregano or marjoram,
  crushed

2 cups chicken or vegetable stock

1 Heat the butter and oil in a heavy-based pan or flameproof casserole. Add the bell peppers and cook until softened.

2 Add the scallions, garlic, rice, and cumin seeds. Cook for about 5 minutes or until the rice turns slightly golden.

3 Add the oregano and stock and bring to a boil. Then reduce the heat and cook for about 5 minutes.

4 Cover with a clean dishtowel and remove from the heat. Leave to steam for about 10 minutes, depending upon the age and maturity of the rice. If the rice is fairly mature, extend the initial cooking time to 10 minutes or longer.

5 Fluff up the rice with a fork and serve.

VARIATIONS

Serve folded through a portion or two of black beans, and serve as a side dish with hearty roasted meat or poultry.

Green Rice

A paste of roasted onions, garlic and chilies, puréed with lots of green cilantro leaves gives this rice a lovely fresh color and stunning taste.

Serves 4

INGREDIENTS

1 onion, halved and unpeeled
6-8 large garlic cloves, unpeeled
1 large mild chili, or 1 green bell
    pepper and 1 small green chili

1 bunch fresh cilantro leaves,
    chopped
1 cup chicken or vegetable stock
1½ cups long-grain rice

⅓ cup vegetable or olive oil
salt and pepper
fresh cilantro sprig, to garnish

1 Heat a heavy-based ungreased frying pan and cook the onion, garlic, chili, and pepper, if using, until lightly charred on all sides, including the cut sides of the onions. Cover and leave to cool.

2 When cool enough to handle, remove the seeds and skin from the chili and bell pepper, if using. Chop the flesh.

3 Remove the skins from the onion and garlic and chop finely.

4 Place the vegetables in a food processor with the cilantro leaves and stock, then process until a smooth thin purée forms.

5 Heat the oil in a heavy-based pan and fry the rice until it is glistening and lightly browned in places, stirring to prevent it from burning. Add the purée, cover and cook over a medium-low heat for 10-15 minutes until the rice is just tender.

6 Fluff up the rice with a fork, then cover and stand for about

5 minutes. Adjust the seasoning, garnish with a sprig of cilantro and serve.

COOK'S TIP

Leftover green rice is delicious mixed with ground beef and/or pork for savory meatballs, or as a filling for cabbage or bell peppers.

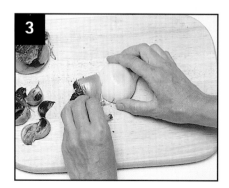

Rice with Black Beans

Any kind of bean cooking liquid is delicious for cooking rice—
black beans are particularly good for their startling gray color and earthy flavor.

Serves 4

INGREDIENTS

1 onion, chopped
5 garlic cloves, chopped
1 cup chicken or vegetable stock
1½ cups long-grain rice
2 tbsp. vegetable oil

½ tsp. ground cumin
1 cup liquid from cooking black beans
  (including some black beans, too)
salt and pepper

TO GARNISH:
3-5 scallions, thinly sliced
2 tbsp. chopped fresh cilantro leaves

1 Put the onion in a blender with the garlic and stock and blend until the consistency of a chunky sauce.

2 Heat the oil in a heavy-based pan and cook the rice until it is golden. Add the onion mixture, with the cooking liquid from the black beans (and any beans, too). Add the cumin, with salt and pepper to taste.

3 Cover and cook over a medium-low heat for about 10 minutes until the rice is just tender. It should be a grayish color and taste delicious.

4 Fluff up the rice with a fork, and leave to rest about 5 minutes, covered. Serve sprinkled with scallions and cilantro.

VARIATIONS

Instead of black beans, use pinto beans or chickpeas. Proceed as above and serve with any savory spicy sauce, or as an accompaniment to roasted meat

Lentils Simmered with Fruit

Although this might seem an unusual combination, when you spoon up this traditional dish you'll see how the fruit lightens the earthy lentils, to create a delicious side dish.

Serves 4

INGREDIENTS

4 ½ oz. brown or green lentils
bout 4 cups water
3 small to medium onions, chopped
4 garlic cloves, coarsely chopped
2 tbsp. vegetable oil
1 large tart apple, roughly chopped

about ¼ ripe pineapple, skin removed
and roughly chopped
3 tomatoes, deseeded and diced
1 almost ripe banana, cut into
bite-sized pieces
salt

cayenne, to taste
fresh parsley sprig, to garnish

1 Combine the lentils with the water in a pan, then bring to a boil. Reduce the heat and simmer over a low heat for about 40 minutes until the lentils are tender. Do not let them get mushy.

2 Meanwhile, heat the oil in a frying pan and fry the onions and garlic until lightly browned and softened. Add the apple and continue to cook until golden.

Add the pineapple, heat through, stirring, then add the tomatoes. Cook over a medium heat until thickened, stirring occasionally.

3 Drain the lentils, reserving 1 cup of the cooking liquid. Add the drained lentils to the sauce, stirring in the reserved liquid if necessary. Heat through to mingle the flavors.

4 Add the banana to the pan, then season with salt and cayenne pepper. Serve garnished with parsley.

VARIATIONS

Instead of lentils, prepare the dish using cooked pinto or cranberry beans.

Dry Soup of Thin Noodles

This curiously named baked dish is made with pasta, tortillas, or rice, and has an appealing dense texture. It often has a cheese topping and is served either as an appetizer or as a comforting supper dish.

Serves 4

INGREDIENTS

12 oz. very thin pasta, such as fideo or capellini

2-3 bay leaves

2-3 chorizo sausages

1 onion, chopped

1 green bell pepper or mild green chili, such as Anaheim or poblano,

deseeded and chopped

4-5 garlic cloves, finely chopped

1½ cups chunky tomato sauce

1½ cups hot chicken, meat or vegetable stock

¼ tsp. ground cumin

½ tsp. mild red chili powder

pinch of dried oregano leaves

12 oz. grated sharp cheese

2 tbsp. chopped fresh cilantro

1 Boil the pasta in boiling salted water with the bay leaves. Drain and discard the bay leaves. Rinse the noodles to rid them of excess starch. Leave to drain.

2 Fry the chorizo in a frying pan. When it begins to brown, add the onion, bell pepper, and garlic, then continue to cook until the vegetables are softened.

3 Add the chunky tomato sauce, stock, cumin, chili, and oregano and remove from the heat.

4 Toss the pasta with the hot sauce, then transfer to an ovenproof dish. Cover with a layer of the grated cheese.

5 Bake in a preheated oven at 400° F for about 15 minutes until the top is lightly browned and the pasta is heated through. Serve immediately, sprinkled with the chopped fresh cilantro.

Main Courses

In Mexico the main meal is traditionally served at mid-day, a gloriously relaxed affair, with usually a fish or meat dish for the central course. Using a wonderful mix of flavors and cooking methods, a result of Mexico's complex and colorful past, the cuisine offers some delicious main dishes, full of spicy tastes.

Eggs are cooked with spices, tangy herbs, garlic, and tomatoes to make an appetizing topping to tortillas, while fish is given a lift with subtle spicy marinades—salmon grilled with a smokey chili dressing or snapper baked with lime and cilantro is a feast of Mexican flavors.

Sizzling strips of beef rolled up with crunchy vegetables in a tortilla is classic Mexican fare, as is pork stewed with mild chilies, sweet plantains, and potatoes—an inspiring marriage of flavors and textures. Or try the classic Mexican way of simmering pork until meltingly tender, then frying it until crisp and golden. Cook chicken with Mexican flair by stewing it with vegetables and fruit, or marinate chicken wings in tequila, to tenderize and add flavor for barbecuing.

Serve any of the dishes in this chapter to bring a touch of sunny Mexico to your meals, whether it is a family lunch or a dinner with friends.

Huevos Tapatios

This hearty breakfast dish from Jalisco is a classic Mexican way of serving eggs—
a feast of flavors!

Serves 4

INGREDIENTS

4 soft corn tortillas	2 tbsp. butter or water, for cooking	1 tbsp. chopped fresh cilantro
1 avocado	4 eggs	1 tbsp. finely chopped scallions
lime or lemon juice, for tossing	4 tbsp. feta cheese, crumbled	
6 oz. chorizo sausage, sliced or diced	salsa of your choice	

1 Heat the tortillas in an ungreased nonstick frying pan, sprinkling them with a few drops of water as they heat; wrap the tortillas in a clean dishtowel as you work to keep them warm. Alternatively, heat through in a stack in the pan, alternating the top and bottom tortillas so that they warm evenly. Wrap to keep warm.

2 Cut the avocado in half around the pit. Twist apart, then remove the pit with a knife. Carefully peel off the skin, dice the flesh and toss in lime or lemon juice to prevent discoloration.

3 Brown the chorizo sausage in a pan, then arrange on each warmed tortilla. Keep warm.

4 Meanwhile, heat the butter or water in a nonstick frying pan, break in an egg and cook until the white is set but the yolk still soft. Remove from the pan and place on top of one tortilla. Keep warm.

5 Cook the remaining eggs in the same way, adding to the tortillas.

6 Arrange the avocado, cheese, and a spoonful of salsa on each tortilla. Add the fresh cilantro and scallions and serve.

Migas

A wonderful brunch or late-night supper dish, this is made by scrambling egg with chilies,
tomatoes, and crisp tortilla chips.

Serves 4

INGREDIENTS

6 garlic cloves, finely chopped
1 fresh green chili, such as jalapeño
   or serrano, deseeded and diced
2 tbsp. butter
1½ tsp. ground cumin

6 ripe tomatoes, coarsely chopped
8 eggs, lightly beaten
8-10 soft corn tortillas, cut into strips
   and fried until crisp, or an equal
   amount of unsalted tortilla chips

4 tbsp. chopped fresh cilantro
3-4 scallions, thinly sliced
mild chili powder, to garnish

1 Melt half the butter in a pan. Add the garlic and chili and cook until softened, but not browned. Add the cumin and cook for 30 seconds, stirring, then add the tomatoes and cook over a medium heat for an additional 3-4 minutes, or until the tomato juices have evaporated. Remove from the pan and set aside.

2 Melt the remaining butter in a frying pan over a low heat and pour in the beaten eggs. Cook, stirring, until the eggs begin to set.

3 Add the reserved chili tomato mixture, stirring gently to mix into the eggs.

4 Carefully add the tortilla strips or chips and continue cooking, stirring once or twice, until the eggs are the consistency you wish. The tortillas should be pliable and chewy.

5 Transfer to a serving plate and surround with the fresh cilantro and spring onions. Garnish with a sprinkling of mild chili powder and serve.

COOK'S TIP

Serve the migas with sour cream or crème fraîche on top, to melt seductively into the spicy eggs.

VARIATIONS

Add browned ground beef or pork to the softly scrambling egg mixture at Step 3. A bunch of cooked, chopped, spinach or chard can be stirred in as well, to add fresh color.

Huevos Oaxaquena

Eggs in the style of Oaxaca. Cooking eggs in a flat omelette, then cutting them into strips and simmering them in a spicy sauce makes an unusual dish for brunch or dinner.

Serves 4

INGREDIENTS

2 lb. 4 oz. ripe tomatoes
about 12 small button onions, halved
8 garlic cloves, whole and unpeeled
2 fresh mild green chilies
pinch of ground cumin

pinch of dried oregano,
pinch of sugar, if needed
2-3 tsp. vegetable oil
8 eggs, lightly beaten
1-2 tbsp. tomato paste

salt and pepper
1-2 tbsp. chopped fresh cilantro, to
   garnish

1 Heat an ungreased heavy-based frying pan, add the tomatoes and char lightly, turning them once or twice. Allow to cool.

2 Meanwhile lightly char the onions, garlic, and chilies in the pan. Allow to cool slightly.

3 Cut the cooled tomatoes into pieces and place in a blender or food processor, with their charred skins. Remove the stems and seeds from the chilies, then peel and chop. Remove the skins from the garlic, then chop. Roughly chop the onions. Add the chilies, garlic, and onions to the tomatoes.

4 Process to make a rough purée, then add the cumin and oregano. Season with salt and pepper to taste, and add sugar if needed.

5 Heat the oil in a heavy-based frying pan, add a ladleful of egg and cook to make a thin omelette. Continue to make omelettes, stacking them on a plate as they are cooked. Slice into noodle-like ribbons.

6 Bring the sauce to a boil, adjust the seasoning, adding tomato paste to taste. Add the omelette strips, warm through and serve at once, garnished with a sprinkling of fresh cilantro.

Huevos with Black Beans

In the Yucatan, this classic dish would be sandwiched between two crisp tortillas,
but layering it all on top of one tortilla looks much more festive.

Serves 4

INGREDIENTS

14 oz. tomatoes, skin and chopped
1 onion, chopped
1 garlic clove, finely chopped
½ fresh green chili, such as jalapeño
   or serrano, deseeded and chopped
¼ tsp. ground cumin
2 tbsp. extra-virgin olive oil
1 plantain, peeled and diced
1 tbsp. butter

4 soft corn tortillas, warmed or fried
   crisply into a tostada
about 14 oz. can refried beans,
   warmed with 2 tbsp. of water
2 tbsp. water or butter
8 eggs
1 red bell pepper, broiled, peeled,
   deseeded and cut into strips
3-4 tbsp. cooked green peas, at room

temperature
4-6 tbsp. diced cooked or smoked
   ham
2-3 oz. crumbled feta cheese
3 scallions, thinly sliced
salt and pepper

1 Place the tomatoes in a blender or food processor with the onion, garlic, chili, cumin, and salt and pepper. Process to a purée.

2 Heat the oil in a heavy-based frying pan, then ladle in a little of the sauce and cook until it reduces in volume and becomes almost paste-like. Continue adding and reducing the sauce in this way. Keep warm.

3 Brown the plantain in the butter in a heavy-based nonstick frying pan. Remove and set aside. Spread the tortillas with the refried beans and keep warm in a low oven.

4 Heat the water or butter in the frying pan, break in an egg and cook until the white is set but the yolk still soft. Remove from the pan and place on top of one tortilla. Cook the remaining eggs in the same way, adding to the tortillas.

5 To serve, spoon the warm sauce around the eggs on each tortilla, sprinkle, with the diced plantain, bell pepper, peas, ham, cheese and scallions. Serve immediately.

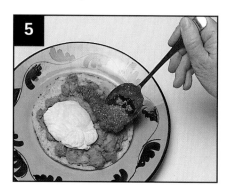

Fish with Yucatecan Flavors

Annatto seeds are rock hard little red seeds that need to be soaked overnight before you can grind them. They have a distinctive lemony flavor and impart a dark orange color to the dish.

Serves 8

INGREDIENTS

4 tbsp. annatto seeds, soaked in water
   overnight
3 garlic cloves, finely chopped
1 tbsp. mild chili powder
1 tbsp. paprika
1 tsp. ground cumin
½ tsp. dried oregano

2 tbsp. beer or tequila
juice of 1 lime and 1 orange or 3 tbsp.
   pineapple juice
2 tbsp. olive oil
2 tbsp. chopped fresh cilantro
¼ tsp. ground cinnamon
¼ tsp. ground cloves

2 lb. 4 oz. swordfish steaks
banana leaves, for wrapping
   (optional)
fresh cilantro leaves, to garnish
orange wedges, to serve

1 Drain the annatto, then crush them to a paste with a mortar and pestle. Work in the garlic, chili powder, paprika, cumin, oregano, beer or tequila, fruit juice, olive oil, fresh cilantro, cinnamon, and cloves.

2 Smear the paste on to the fish and marinate in the refrigerator for at least 3 hours or overnight.

3 Wrap the fish steak in banana leaves, tying with string to make packages. Bring water to a boil in a steamer, then add a batch packages to the top part of the steamer and cook for about 15 minutes or until the fish is cooked through.

4 Alternatively, cook the fish without wrapping in the banana leaves. To cook on the grill, place in a hinged basket, or on a rack, and cook over the hot coals for 5-6 minutes on each side until cooked through. Or cook the fish under a preheated broiler for 5-6 minutes on each side until cooked through.

5 Garnish with cilantro and serve with orange wedges for squeezing over the fish.

Shrimp in Green Bean Sauce

*The sweet briny flesh of shrimp is wonderful paired
with the smoky scent of chipotle chili.*

Serves 4

INGREDIENTS

3 onions, chopped
5 garlic cloves, chopped
2 tbsp. vegetable oil
5-7 ripe tomatoes, diced
6-8 oz. green beans, cut into 2 inch
   pieces and blanched in boiling
   water for 1 minute
¼ tsp. ground cumin

pinch of ground allspice
pinch of ground cinnamon
½-1 canned chipotle chili in adobo
   marinade, with some of the
   marinade
2 cups fish stock or water mixed with
   a fish stock cube
1 lb. raw shrimp, peeled

fresh cilantro sprigs
1 lime, cut into wedges

1 Lightly fry the onion and garlic in the oil over a low heat for 5-10 minutes until softened. Add the tomatoes and cook an additional 2 minutes.

2 Add the green beans, cumin, allspice, cinnamon, the chipotle chili, and marinade and fish stock. Bring to a boil, then reduce the heat and simmer for a few minutes to combine the flavors.

3 Add the shrimp and cook for 1-2 minutes only, then remove the pan from the heat and leave the shrimp to steep in the hot liquid to finish cooking. They are cooked when they have turned bright pink.

4 Serve immediately, garnished with the fresh cilantro and accompanied by the lime wedges.

VARIATIONS

*If you can find them, use
bottled nopales (edible
cactus), cut into strips, to add
an exotic touch to the dish.*

Mussels Cooked with Lager

Mussels cooked in beer, tomatoes, and Mexican spices are great summertime fare.

Serves 4

INGREDIENTS

3 lb. 5 oz. live mussels
2 cups lager
2 onions, chopped
5 garlic cloves, chopped coarsely

1 fresh green chili, such as jalapeño or serrano, deseeded and thinly sliced
²/₃ cup fresh tomatoes, diced, or

canned chopped
2-3 tbsp. chopped fresh cilantro

1 Scrub the mussels under cold running water to remove any mud. Using a sharp knife, cut away the feathery "beards" from the shells. Discard any open mussels that do not shut when tapped sharply with a knife. Rinse again in cold water.

2 Place the lager, onions, garlic, chili, and tomatoes in a heavy-based pan. Bring to a boil.

3 Add the mussels and cook, covered, over a medium-high heat for about 10 minutes until the shells open. Discard any mussels that do not open.

4 Ladle into individual bowls and serve sprinkled with fresh cilantro.

VARIATIONS

Add the kernels from 2 ears of corn to the lager mixture in Step 2. A pinch of sugar might be needed to bring out the sweetness of the corn.

Barbecued Clams with Corn Salsa

Cook with Mexican flair, and serve up clams from the grill, topped with a spicy corn salsa.

Serves 4

INGREDIENTS

4 lb. 8 oz. lb. clams in their shells

5 ripe tomatoes

2 garlic cloves, finely chopped

8 oz. can corn, drained

3 tbsp. finely chopped fresh cilantro

3 scallions, thinly sliced

¼ tsp. ground cumin

juice of ½ lime

½-1 fresh green chili, deseeded and finely chopped

salt

lime wedges, to serve

1 Place the clams in a large bowl. Cover with cold water and add a handful of salt. Leave to soak for 30 minutes to rinse out the sand and grit.

2 Meanwhile, skin the tomatoes. Place in a heatproof bowl, pour boiling water over to cover and stand for 30 seconds. Drain and plunge into cold water. The skins will then slide off easily. Cut the tomatoes in half, deseed, then chop the flesh.

3 To make the salsa, combine the tomatoes, garlic, corn, coriander, scallions, cumin, lime juice, and chili in a bowl. Season with salt to taste.

4 Drain the clams, discarding any that are open. Place the clams on the hot coals of a barbecue, allowing about 5 minutes per side. They will pop open when they are ready.

5 Immediately remove from the barbecue, top with the salsa and serve with lime wedges for squeezing over the clams.

VARIATIONS

Mussels can be used in place of the clams very successfully.

Chili-marinated Shrimp with Avocado Sauce

Avocado salsa is delicious spooned on to anything spicy from the broiler or barbecue, especially seafood.

Serves 4

INGREDIENTS

1 lb. 5 oz. large shrimp, shelled

½ tsp. ground cumin

½ tsp. mild chili powder

½ tsp. paprika

2 tbsp. orange juice

grated rind of 1 orange

2 tbsp. extra-virgin olive oil

2 tbsp. chopped fresh cilantro, plus extra for garnishing

1 ripe avocado

½ onion, finely chopped

¼ fresh green or red chili, deseeded and chopped

juice of ½ lime

salt and pepper

1 Combine the shrimp with the cumin, chili, paprika, orange juice and rind, olive oil, and half the fresh cilantro. Add salt and pepper to taste.

2 Thread the shrimp on to metal skewers, or bamboo skewers that have been soaked in cold water for 30 minutes.

3 Cut the avocado in half around the pit. Twist apart, then remove the pit with a knife. Carefully peel off the skin, dice the flesh. Immediately combine the avocado with the remaining cilantro, onion, chili, and lime juice. Season with salt and pepper and set aside.

4 Place the shrimp on a hot barbecue and cook for only a few minutes on each side.

5 Serve the shrimp, garnished with cilantro and accompanied by the avocado sauce.

VARIATIONS

Big juicy spiced shrimp make the most luscious of sandwiches. Toast rolls, cut in half and buttered, over the hot coals and fill them with the cooked shrimp and avocado sauce.

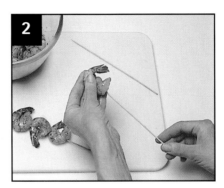

Squid Simmered with Tomatoes, Olives, and Capers

This flavorful squid dish from Vera Cruz would be good with warmed flour tortillas, for do-it-yourself tacos.

Serves 4

INGREDIENTS

3 tbsp. extra-virgin olive oil
2 lb. cleaned squid, cut into rings and
    tentacles
1 onion, chopped
3 garlic cloves, chopped
14 oz. can chopped tomatoes
½-1 fresh mildish green chili,

deseeded and chopped
1 tbsp. finely chopped fresh parsley
¼ tsp. chopped fresh thyme
¼ tsp. chopped fresh oregano
¼ tsp. chopped fresh marjoram
large pinch of ground cinnamon
large pinch of ground allspice

large pinch of sugar
15-20 pimiento-stuffed green olives,
    sliced
1 tbsp. capers
salt and pepper
1 tbsp. chopped fresh cilantro, to
    garnish

1 Heat the oil in a pan and lightly fry the squid until it turns opaque. Season with salt and pepper and remove from the pan with a slotted spoon.

2 Add the onion and garlic to the remaining oil in the pan and fry until softened. Stir in the tomatoes, chilies, herbs, cinnamon, allspice, sugar, and olives. Cover and cook over a medium-low heat for 5-10 minutes until the mixture thickens slightly. Uncover the pan and cook for an additional 5 minutes to concentrate the flavors.

3 Stir in the reserved squid and any of the juices that have gathered. Add the capers and heat through.

4 Adjust the seasoning, then serve immediately, garnished with fresh cilantro.

Pan-fried Scallops Mexicana

Scallops, with their sweet flesh, are delicious with the flavors of Mexico. Often they are prepared just this simply, served with wedges of lime to squeeze over as desired, and a stack of warm corn tortillas.

Serves 4–6

INGREDIENTS

2 tbsp. butter

2 tbsp. extra-virgin olive oil

1 lb. 6 oz. scallops, shelled

4–5 scallions, thinly sliced

3–4 garlic cloves, finely chopped

½ fresh green chili, deseeded and finely chopped

2 tbsp. finely chopped fresh cilantro

juice of ½ lime

salt and pepper

lime wedges, to serve

1 Heat half the butter and olive oil in a heavy-based frying pan until the butter foams, then add the scallops and cook quickly until just turning opaque; do not overcook. Remove from the pan with a slotted spoon and keep warm.

2 Add the remaining butter and oil to the pan, then toss in the scallions and garlic and cook over a medium heat until the scallions wilt. Return the scallops to the pan.

3 Remove the pan from the heat and add the chili, cilantro, and lime juice. Season with salt and pepper and stir to mix well.

4 Serve immediately with lime wedges for squeezing over the scallops.

VARIATIONS

Mix leftover scallops with a little aioli or mayonnaise mixed with garlic and a little olive oil. Serve with roasted bell peppers on a bed of greens, with a handful of salty black olives for a taste of the Mediterranean, Mexico style.

Mexican-style Salmon

The woody smoked flavors of the chipotle chili are delicious brushed onto salmon for grilling.

Serves 4

INGREDIENTS

4 salmon steaks, about 6-8 oz. each
lime slices, to garnish

MARINADE:
4 garlic cloves, finely chopped
2 tbsp. extra-virgin olive oil
pinch of ground allspice
pinch of ground cinnamon

juice of 2 limes
1-2 tsp. marinade from canned
  chipotle chilies or bottled chipotle
  chili salsa
¼ tsp. ground cumin
pinch of sugar
salt and pepper

TO SERVE:
tomato wedges
3 scallions finely chopped
shredded lettuce

1 To make the marinade, finely chop the garlic and place in a bowl with the olive oil, allspice, cinnamon, lime juice, chipotle marinade, cumin, and sugar. Add salt and pepper and stir to combine.

2 Coat the salmon with the garlic mixture, then place in a nonmetallic dish. Leave to marinate for at least an hour or overnight in the refrigerator.

3 Transfer to a broiler pan and cook under a preheated broiler for 3-4 minutes on each side. Alternatively, cook the salmon over hot coals on a grill until cooked through.

4 To serve, mix the tomato wedges with the scallions. Place the salmon on individual plates and arrange the tomato salad and shredded lettuce alongside. Garnish with lime slices and serve.

VARIATION

The marinade also goes well with fresh tuna steaks.

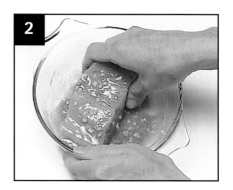

Fish Baked with Lime

Tangy and simple to prepare, this is excellent served with rice and beans for an easy lunch. Follow up with coffee ice cream topped with espresso beans and chocolate sauce.

Serves 4

INGREDIENTS

2 lb. 4 oz. white fish fillets, such as
   bass, flounder, or cod
1 lime, halved
3 tbsp. extra-virgin olive oil
1 large onion, finely chopped

3 garlic cloves, finely chopped
2-3 pickled jalapeño chilies (see
   Cook's Tip), chopped
6-8 tbsp. chopped fresh cilantro
salt and pepper

lemon and lime wedges, to serve

1 Place the fish fillets in a bowl and sprinkle with salt and pepper. Squeeze the juice from the lime over the fish.

2 Heat the olive oil in a frying pan. Add the onion and garlic and fry for about 2 minutes, stirring frequently, until softened. Remove from the heat.

3 Place a third of the onion mixture and a little of the chilies and cilantro in the bottom of a shallow baking dish or roasting pan. Arrange the fish on

top. Top with the remaining onion mixture, chilies and cilantro.

4 Bake in a preheated oven at 350° F for about 15-20 minutes or until the fish has become slightly opaque and firm to the touch. Serve at once, with lemon and lime wedges for squeezing over the fish.

COOK'S TIP

Pickled jalapeños are called jalapeños en escabeche and are available from specialty stores.

VARIATIONS

Add sliced flavorful fresh tomatoes, or canned chopped tomatoes, to the onion mixture at the end of Step 2.

Lobster Cooked Beach Style

*Grilling gives lobsters a lovely smoky scent that is enhanced by spicy red chili.
Serve with creamy refried beans and a stack of warm corn tortillas and
pretend you're on Rosarita Beach in Baja California!*

Serves 4

INGREDIENTS

2-4 cooked lobsters, depending on
their size, cut through the middle
into two halves, or 4 lobster tails,
the meat loosened slightly from its
shell

CHILI BUTTER:
4 oz. unsalted butter, softened
3-4 tbsp. chopped fresh cilantro
about 5 garlic cloves, chopped
2-3 tbsp. mild chili powder
juice of ½ lime
salt and pepper

TO SERVE:
14 oz. refried beans, warmed with 2
tbsp. water
chopped scallions
lime wedges
salsa of your choice

1 To make the chili butter, put the butter in a bowl and mix in the cilantro, garlic, chili powder, and lime juice. Add salt and pepper.

2 Rub the chili butter into the cut side of the lobster or the lobster tails, working it into all the lobsters cracks and crevices.

3 Wrap loosely in aluminum foil and place, cut-side up, on a rack over the hot coals of a barbecue. Cook for 15 minutes or until heated through.

4 Serve with warm refried beans, topped with chopped scallions, plus lime wedges and salsa.

COOK'S TIP

*The flavored butter is also
delicious with grilled fish steaks
and large shrimp.*

Ropa Vieja

Fill warmed tortillas with this tender, browned beef and a selection of crisp vegetables to make wonderful tacos.

Serves 6

INGREDIENTS

3 lb. 5 oz. flank beef steak or other
   stewing meat
beef stock
1 carrot, sliced
10 garlic cloves, sliced
2 tbsp. vegetable oil
2 onions, thinly sliced

3-4 mild fresh green chilies, such as
   Anaheim or poblano, deseeded and
   sliced
warmed flour tortillas, to serve

SALAD GARNISHES:
3 ripe tomatoes, diced
8-10 radishes, diced
3-4 tbsp. chopped fresh cilantro
4-5 scallions, chopped
1-2 limes, cut into wedges

1 Put the meat in a large pan and cover with a mixture of stock and water. Add the carrot and half the garlic with salt and pepper to taste. Cover and bring to a boil, then reduce the heat to low. Skim the fat from the surface, then re-cover the pan and cook the meat gently for about 2 hours until very tender.

2 Remove the pan from the heat and leave the meat to cool in the liquid. When cool enough to handle, remove from the liquid and shred with your fingers and a fork.

3 Heat the oil in a large frying pan, add the remaining garlic, onions, and chilies and fry until lightly colored. Remove from the pan and set aside.

4 Add the meat to the pan and cook over a medium-high heat until browned and crisp. Transfer to a serving dish. Top with the onion mixture and surround with the tomatoes, radishes, cilantro, scallions, and lime wedges. Serve with warmed tortillas.

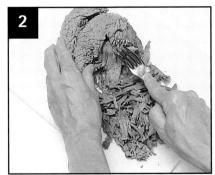

Classic Fajitas

Sizzling marinated strips of meat, rolled up in soft flour tortillas with a tangy salsa is a real Mexican treat, perfect for relaxed entertaining.

Serves 4–6

INGREDIENTS

1 lb. 9 oz. beef skirt steak or other
   tender steak, cut into strips
6 garlic cloves, chopped
juice of 1 lime
large pinch of mild chili powder
large pinch of paprika
large pinch of ground cumin
1–2 tbsp. extra-virgin olive oil
12 flour tortillas

vegetable oil, for frying
1–2 avocados, pitted, sliced and
   tossed with lime juice
½ cup sour cream
salt and pepper

PICO DE GALLO SALSA:
8 ripe tomatoes, diced
3 scallions, thinly sliced

1–2 fresh green chilies, such as
   jalapeño or serrano, deseeded and
   chopped
3–4 tbsp. chopped fresh cilantro
5–8 radishes, diced
ground cumin

1 Combine the beef with half the garlic, half the lime juice, the chili powder, paprika, cumin, and olive oil. Add salt and pepper, mix well and leave to marinate for at least 30 minutes at room temperature, or up to overnight in the refrigerator.

2 To make the pico de gallo salsa, put the tomatoes in a bowl with the scallions, green chili, coriander and radishes. Season to taste with cumin, salt and pepper. Set aside.

3 Heat the tortillas in a lightly greased nonstick frying pan; wrap in aluminum foil as you work, to keep them warm.

4 Stir-fry the meat in a little oil over a high heat until browned and just cooked through.

5 Serve the sizzling hot meat with the warm tortillas, the pico de gallo salsa, avocado, and sour cream for each person to make his or her own rolled up fajitas.

COOK'S TIP

A lettuce and orange salad makes a refreshing accompaniment.

Michoacan Beef

This rich smoky flavored stew is delicious; leftovers
make a great filling for tacos, too!

Serves 4

INGREDIENTS

about 3 tbsp. all-purpose flour

2 lb. 4 oz. stewing beef, cut into large
   bite-sized pieces

2 tbsp. vegetable oil

2 onions, chopped

5 garlic cloves, chopped

14 oz. tomatoes, diced

1½ dried chipotle chilies,

reconstituted (see page 100),
deseeded and cut into thin strips, or
a few shakes of bottled chipotle
salsa

6¼ cups beef stock

12 oz. green beans, topped and tailed

a pinch of sugar

salt and pepper

TO SERVE:
simmered beans
cooked rice

1 Place the flour in a large bowl and season with salt and pepper. Add the beef and toss to coat well. Remove from the bowl, shaking off the excess flour.

2 Heat the oil in a frying pan and brown the meat briefly over a high heat. Reduce the heat to medium, add the onions and garlic and cook for a further 2 minutes.

3 Add the tomatoes, chilies, and stock, then cover and simmer over a low heat for 1½ hours or until the meat is very tender, adding the green beans 15 minutes before the end of the cooking time. Skim off any fat that rises to the surface.

4 Transfer to individual bowls and serve with beans and rice.

COOK'S TIP

This is traditionally made with nopales, edible cactus, which gives the dish a distinctive flavor. Look out for them in specialty stores. For this recipe you need a 12-14 oz. can of nopales, or fresh nopales, peeled, blanched, sliced. Add them with the tomatoes at Step 3.

Chiles Rellenos con Picadillo

Large mildish-tasting green chilies are roasted, peeled and stuffed with a
succulent meat mixture that is sweet, spicy and punctuated with nuts.

Serves 4

INGREDIENTS

4 large fresh mild green chilies	14 oz. can chopped tomatoes	3 eggs, separated
1 1b 2 oz. ground beef	1-3 tsp. sugar	½ cup water
1 onion, finely chopped	1 tbsp. vinegar	salt and pepper
2-3 garlic cloves, finely chopped	3 tbsp. chopped fresh cilantro	vegetable oil, for frying
¼ cup dry or sweet sherry	2-3 tbsp. coarsely chopped toasted	Quick Tomato Sauce (see page 82),
pinch of ground cinnamon	almonds	to serve
pinch of ground cloves	6-8 tbsp. all-purpose flour, plus extra	
pinch of ground cumin	for dusting	

1 Roast the chilies under a preheated broiler until the skin is charred. Place in a plastic bag, seal well and leave to stand for 20 minutes. Make a slit in the side of each chili and remove the seeds, leaving the stems intact. Set aside.

2 Brown the meat and onion together in a heavy-based frying pan over a medium heat.

Pour off any extra fat, then add the garlic and sherry and boil down until it has nearly evaporated.

3 Season with salt, pepper, cinnamon, cloves and cumin, then add the tomatoes, sugar and vinegar and cook over a medium heat until the tomatoes have reduced into a thick, strongly flavored sauce.

4 Stir in the cilantro and almonds and heat through. This is the picadillo mixture. Stuff as much of the picadillo into the chilies as will fit, then dust each with flour. Set aside.

5 Lightly beat the yolks with the flour, a pinch of salt and the water. Whisk the egg whites until they form stiff peaks. Fold the egg whites into the yolk mixture, then gently dip each stuffed chili into the batter.

6 Heat oil in a deep frying pan until very hot, just smoking, and gently fry the chilies until golden. Serve hot, topped with a mild tomato sauce.

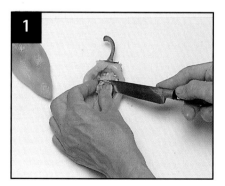

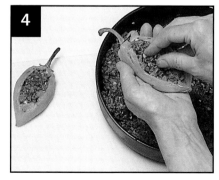

Spicy Pork with Prunes

Prunes add an earthy, wine flavor to this spicy stew.
Serve with crusty bread to dip into the rich sauce.

Serves 4–6

INGREDIENTS

3 lb. 5 oz. pork joint, such as leg or
   shoulder
juice of 2-3 limes
10 garlic cloves, chopped
3-4 tbsp. mild chili powder, such as
   ancho or New Mexico
2 tbsp. vegetable oil

2 onions, chopped
2 ¼ cups chicken stock
25 small tart tomatoes, roughly
   chopped
25 prunes, pitted
1-2 tsp. sugar
about a pinch of ground cinnamon

about a pinch of ground allspice
about a pinch of ground cumin
salt
warmed corn tortillas, to serve

1 Combine the pork with the lime juice, garlic, chili powder, and salt. Leave to marinate in the refrigerator overnight.

2 Remove the pork from marinade and wipe dry with paper towels. Reserve the marinade. Heat the oil in a flameproof casserole and brown the pork evenly until just golden. Add the onions, the reserved marinade and stock. Cover and cook in a preheated oven at 350° F for about 2-3 hours until very tender.

3 Spoon off fat from the surface of the cooking liquid and add the tomatoes. Continue to cook for about 20 minutes until the tomatoes are tender. Mash the tomatoes into a coarse purée. Add the prunes and sugar, then adjust the seasoning, adding cinnamon, allspice and cumin to taste, as well as extra chili powder, if wished.

4 Increase the oven temperature to 400° F and return the meat to the oven for 20-30 minutes or until the meat has browned on top and the juices have thickened.

5 Remove the meat from the pan, stand for a few minute, then carve it into thin slices. Spoon the sauce over and serve with corn tortillas.

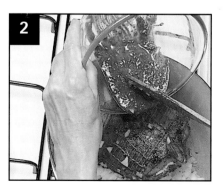

Red Mole of Pork & Red Chillies

Plantain and sesame seeds add a delicious hint of sweetness to this fragrant stew of pork and mild chilies, while potatoes add a satisfying chunky texture.

Serves 6

INGREDIENTS

2 lb. 12 oz. pork shoulder or lean belly, cut into bite-sized pieces
1 onion, chopped
1 whole garlic bulb
2 bay leaves
1-2 stock cubes
6 dried ancho chilies,
6 guajillo chilies

3-5 ripe big flavorful tomatoes
¼ tsp. ground cloves
¼ tsp. ground allspice
1 cinnamon stick
4 tbsp. sesame seeds, toasted
1 large ripe plantain or banana, peeled and diced
3 tbsp. vegetable oil

6-8 waxy potatoes, cut into chunks
3 tbsp. yerba santa, or a combination of chopped fresh mint, oregano and cilantro
salt and pepper

1 Put the pork in a pan with the onion, the garlic, bay leaves, and salt and pepper. Fill to the top.

2 Bring to a boil, then reduce the heat to a slow simmer. Skim off the fat, then stir in the stock cubes and cook the meat, covered, for about 3 hours until very tender.

3 Meanwhile, lightly roast the chilies in an ungreased heavy-based frying pan until they just change color. Put them in a bowl and cover with boiling water. Cover and leave for 20-30 minutes.

4 Roast the tomatoes in the frying pan, then place them under a hot broiler to lightly char the tops. Leave to cool.

5 When the chilies are softened, remove the stems and seeds, then purée them with enough liquid to make a paste. Add the roasted tomatoes, cloves and allspice, with two-thirds of the sesame seeds and the plantain. Purée until smooth.

6 Remove the meat from the pan and reserve. Skim the fat from the surface of the stock.

7 Heat the oil in a pan, add the tomato purée mixture and cook for 10 minutes. Add the potatoes and the yerba santa or herbs, with some stock. Add the cinnamon stick.

8 Cook, covered, until the potatoes are tender. Add the reserved meat and heat through. Serve sprinkled with sesame seeds.

Chile Verde

*If tomatillos are not available, use fresh tomatoes and bottled green salsa instead,
and add a good hit of lime juice at the end.*

Serves 4

INGREDIENTS

2 lb. 4 oz. pork, cut into bite-sized chunks

1 onion, chopped

2 bay leaves

1 whole garlic bulb, cut in half

1 stock cube

2 garlic cloves, chopped

1 lb. oz. fresh tomatillos, husks removed, cooked in a small amount

of water until just tender, then chopped, or canned

2 large fresh mild green chilies, such as Anaheim, or a combination of 1 green bell pepper and 2 jalapeño chilies, deseeded and chopped

3 tbsp. vegetable oil

1 cup pork or chicken stock

½ tsp. mild chili powder, such as

ancho or New Mexico

½ tsp. cumin

4-6 tbsp. chopped fresh cilantro, to garnish

TO SERVE:
warmed flour tortillas
lime wedges

1 Place the pork in a large pan with the onion, bay leaves and garlic bulb. Add water to cover and bring to a boil. Skim off the scum from the surface, reduce the heat to very low and simmer gently for about 1½ hours or until the meat is very tender.

2 Meanwhile, put the chopped garlic in a blender or food processor with the tomatillos and green chilies and pepper, if using. Process to a purée.

3 Heat the oil in a pan, add the tomatillo mixture and cook over a medium-high heat for about 10 minutes or until thickened. Add the stock, chili powder, and cumin.

4 When the meat is tender, remove from the pan and add to the sauce. Simmer gently to combine the flavors.

5 Garnish with the chopped cilantro and serve with warmed tortillas and lime wedges

Meatballs in Spicy-sweet Sauce

Called albondigas in Mexican, these tasty meatballs are set off brilliantly against the rich sauce and golden sweet potatoes.

Serves 4

INGREDIENTS

8 oz. ground pork

8 oz. ground beef or lamb

6 tbsp. cooked rice or finely crushed tortilla chips

1 egg, lightly beaten

1½ onions, finely chopped

5 garlic cloves, finely chopped

½ tsp. ground cumin

large pinch of ground cinnamon

2 tbsp. raisins

1 tbsp. dark brown sugar

1-2 tbsp. cider or wine vinegar

14 oz. can tomatoes, drained and chopped

12 fl oz. beef stock

1-2 tbsp. mild chili or ancho chili powder

1 tbsp. paprika

1 tbsp. chopped fresh cilantro

1 tbsp. chopped fresh parsley or mint

2 tbsp. vegetable oil

2 sweet potatoes, peeled and cut into small bite-sized chunks

salt and pepper

grated cheese, to serve

1 Mix the meat with the rice or crushed tortilla chips, the egg, half the onion, half the garlic, the cumin, cinnamon, and raisins.

2 Divide the mixture into even-sized pieces and roll into balls. Fry the balls in a nonstick frying pan over a medium heat, adding a tiny bit of oil, if necessary, to help them brown. Remove from the pan and set aside.

3 Place the brown sugar in a blender or food processor, with the vinegar, tomatoes, stock, chili powder, paprika, and remaining onion and garlic. Process, then stir in the chopped fresh herbs. Set aside.

4 Heat the oil in the cleaned frying pan, add the sweet potatoes and cook until tender and golden. Pour in the blended sauce

and add the meatballs. Cook for about 10 minutes until the meatballs are heated through and the flavors have combined. Season with salt and pepper. Serve accompanied by grated cheese.

Carnitas

In this classic Mexican dish, pieces of pork are first simmered to make them meltingly tender, then browned until irresistibly crisp.

Serves 4

INGREDIENTS

2 lb. 4 oz. pork, such as lean belly
1 onion, chopped
1 whole garlic bulb, cut into half
½ tsp. ground cumin
2 meat stock cubes

2 bay leaves vegetable oil, for frying
about 3 tbsp. meat stock, if needed
salt and pepper
fresh chili strips, to garnish

TO SERVE:
cooked rice
refried beans (see page 144)
salsa of your choice

1 Place the pork in a heavy-based pan with the onion, garlic, cumin, stock cubes, and bay leaves. Add water to cover. Bring to a boil, then reduce the heat to very low. Skim off the foam and fat that has formed on the surface of the liquid.

2 Continue to cook very gently for about 2 hours or until the meat is tender. Remove from the heat and leave the meat to cool in the liquid.

3 Remove the meat from the pan with a slotted spoon. Cut off any rind (roast separately to make crackling). Cut the meat into bite-sized pieces and sprinkle with salt and pepper.

4 Brown the meat in a heavy-based frying pan for about 30 minutes, covering the pan as the meat cooks, to render out the fat and turn it crispy. Turn the meat every now and again. If the meat looks dry about halfway through

the cooking time, add a few tablespoons of stock.

5 Transfer the meat to a serving dish, garnish with chili strips and serve with rice, refried beans, and salsa.

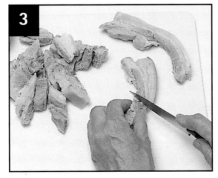

Spicy Meat
& Chipotle Hash

*This specialty from the town of Puebla in Mexico makes divine soft tacos: simply
serve with a stack of warm soft corn tortillas and let everyone roll their own, fajita-style.*

Serves 4

INGREDIENTS

1 onion, finely chopped

1 tbsp. vegetable oil

1 tbsp. mild chili powder

1 lb. leftover meat, such as simmered
   pork or beef, cooled and cut into
   thin strips

2 ripe tomatoes, deseeded and diced

about 1 cup meat stock

½-1 canned chipotle chilies, mashed,
   plus a little of the marinade, or a
   few shakes bottled chipotle salsa

½ cup sour cream

4-6 tbsp. chopped fresh cilantro

4-6 tbsp. chopped radishes

3-4 leaves crisp lettuce, such as
   romaine, shredded

1 Heat the oil in a frying pan,
add the onion and cook until
softened, stirring occasionally.
Add the meat and sauté for about
3 minutes, stirring, until lightly
browned.

2 Add the chili powder,
tomatoes, and stock and cook
until the tomatoes reduce to a
sauce; mash the meat a bit as it
cooks.

3 Add the chipotle chilies and
continue to cook and mash
until the sauce and meat are nearly
blended.

4 Serve the dish with a stack of
warmed corn tortillas so that
people can fill them with the
meaty mixture to make tacos. Also
serve sour cream, fresh cilantro,
radishes, and lettuce for each
person to add to the meat.

COOK'S TIP

*Avocados add an
interesting texture
contrast to the
spicy meat—serve with 2 sliced
avocados, tossed with lime juice.
Try serving on top of tostada,
crisply fried tortillas, instead of
wrapping taco-style.*

Simmered Stew of Meat, Chicken, Vegetables, & Fruit

A big pot of cocido is warming on a cold day, great for a family meal. Serve with a selection of several salsas, a stack of corn tortillas, and a bowl of rice.

Serves 6-8

INGREDIENTS

2 lb. boneless pork, either in one joint
   or in pieces
2 bay leaves
1 onion, chopped
8 garlic cloves, finely chopped
2 tbsp. chopped fresh cilantro
1 carrot, thinly sliced
2 sticks celery, diced
2 chicken stock cubes

½ chicken, cut into portions
4-5 ripe tomatoes, diced
½ tsp. mild chili powder
grated rind of ¼ orange
¼ tsp. ground cumin
juice of 3 oranges
1 zucchini, cut into bite-sized pieces
¼ cabbage, thinly sliced and blanched
1 apple, cut into bite-sized pieces

about 10 prunes, pitted
¼ tsp. ground cinnamon
pinch of dried ginger
2 hard chorizo sausages, about 12 oz.
   in total, cut into bite-sized pieces
salt and pepper

1 Combine the pork, bay leaves, onion, garlic, cilantro, carrot, and celery in a large pan and fill with cold water to the top. Bring to a boil, skim off the scum that has formed on the surface, then reduce heat and simmer gently for an hour.

2 Add the stock cubes to the pan, along with the chicken, tomatoes, chili powder, orange rind, and cumin. Continue to cook for a further 45 minutes or until the chicken is tender. Spoon off the fat that forms on the top of the liquid.

3 Add the orange juice, zucchini, cabbage, apple, prunes, cinnamon, ginger, and chorizo.

Continue to simmer for a further 20 minutes or until the zucchini is tender and the chorizo cooked through.

4 Season with salt and pepper and serve at once.

Chicken Breasts in Green Salsa with Sour Cream

Chicken breasts bathed in a fragrant sauce make a delicate dish, perfect for dinner parties. Serve with rice to complete the meal.

Serves 4

INGREDIENTS

4 chicken breast fillets
flour, for dredging
2-3 tbsp. butter or combination
   butter and oil
1 lb. mild green salsa or
   puréed tomatillos
1 cup chicken stock

1-2 garlic cloves, finely chopped
3-5 tbsp. chopped fresh cilantro
½ fresh green chili, deseeded and
   chopped
½ tsp. ground cumin
salt and pepper

TO SERVE:
1 cup sour cream
several leaves romaine lettuce,
   shredded
3-5 scallions, thinly sliced
coarsely chopped fresh cilantro

1 Sprinkle the chicken with salt and pepper, then dredge in flour. Shake off the excess.

2 Melt the butter in a frying pan, add the chicken and cook over a medium heat-high, turning once, until they are golden but not cooked through—they will continue to cook slightly in the sauce. Remove from pan and set aside.

3 Place the salsa, chicken stock, garlic, cilantro, chili, and cumin in a pan and bring to a boil. Reduce the heat to a low simmer. Add the chicken breasts to the sauce, spooning the sauce over the chicken. Continue to cook until the chicken is cooked through.

4 Remove the chicken from the pan and season with salt and pepper. Serve with the sour cream, shredded lettuce, scallions, and fresh cilantro leaves.

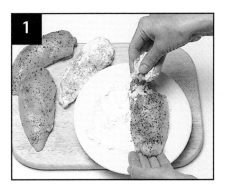

Chicken Thighs with Yucatecan-flavored Vinegar Sauce

A paste of roasted garlic and mixed spices gives its evocative flavor to this tangy dish.

Serves 4–6

INGREDIENTS

8 small boned chicken thighs
chicken stock
15-20 garlic cloves, unpeeled
1 tsp. cumin seeds
1 tsp. coarsely ground black pepper
½ tsp. ground cloves
2 tsp. crumbled dried oregano or ½

tsp. crushed or powdered bay
 leaves
about ½ tsp. salt
1 tbsp. lime juice
1 tbsp. flour, plus extra for dredging
 the chicken
3-4 onions, thinly sliced

2 fresh chilies, preferably mildish
 yellow ones, such as Mexican Guero
 or similar Turkish or Greek chilies,
 deseeded and sliced
1 cup vegetable oil
scant ½ cup cider or sherry vinegar

1 Place the chicken in a pan with enough stock to cover. Bring to a boil, then reduce the heat and simmer for 5 minutes. Remove from the heat and allow the chicken to cool in the stock; the chicken will continue to cook as it cools in the hot stock.

2 Meanwhile, roast the garlic cloves in an ungreased heavy-based nonstick frying pan until lightly browned. Remove from

the heat. When cool, squeeze the flesh and place in a bowl.

3 Lightly toast the cumin seeds in the ungreased nonstick frying pan until they are fragrant; take care not to burn. Set aside.

4 Grind the garlic with the pepper, cloves, oregano, salt, lime juice, and three-quarters of the cumin seeds. Mix with the flour. When the chicken is cool,

remove from the stock and pat dry. Rub the chicken with about two-thirds of the garlic-spice paste and stand at room temperature for at least 30 minutes or up to overnight in the refrigerator.

5 Fry the onions and chilies in a tiny bit of the oil until golden and softened. Pour in the vinegar and remaining cumin seeds, cook for a few minutes, then add the reserved stock and remaining spice paste. Boil, stirring, for about 10 minutes until reduced in volume.

6 Dredge the chicken in flour. Heat the remaining oil in a heavy-based frying pan. Fry the chicken until lightly browned, then remove and serve topped with the onion and vinegar sauce.

Tequila-marinated Crisp Chicken Wings

The tequila tenderizes these tasty chiken wings and gives them a delicious flavour. Serve as part of a barbecue, accompanied by corn tortillas, refried beans, salsa, and lots of chilled lager.

Serves 4

INGREDIENTS

2 lb chicken wings
11 garlic cloves, finely chopped
juice of 2 limes
juice of 1 orange
2 tbsp. tequila

1 tbsp. mild chili powder
2 tsp. Chipotle Salsa (see page 98)
   or 2 dried chipotle chillies,
   reconstituted (see page 100) and
   pureéd
2 tbsp. vegetable oil

1 tsp. sugar
¼ tsp. ground allspice
pinch of ground cinnamon
pinch of ground cumin
pinch of dried oregano

1 Cut the chicken wings into two pieces at the joint.

2 Place the chicken wing in a non-metallic dish and add the remaining ingredients. Toss well to coat, then leave to marinate for at least 3 hours or overnight in the refrigerator.

3 Cook over the hot coals of a grill for about 15–20 minutes or until the wings are crisply browned, turning occasionally. To test whether the chicken is cooked, pierce a thick part with a skewer – the juices should run clear. Serve at once.

COOK'S TIP

Made from the agave plant, tequila is Mexico's famous alcoholic drink.

Citrus-Marinated Chicken

This is a great dish for a summer meal. The marinade gives the chicken an appetizing flavor and helps keeps it succulent and moist during cooking.

Serves 4

INGREDIENTS

1 chicken, cut into 4 pieces
1 tbsp. mild chili powder
1 tbsp. paprika
2 tsp. ground cumin
juice and rind of 1 orange
juice of 3 limes
pinch of sugar
8-10 garlic cloves, finely chopped

1 bunch fresh cilantro, coarsely
  chopped
2-3 tbsp. extra-virgin olive oil
½ cup beer, tequila, or pineapple juice
  (optional)
salt and pepper
fresh cilantro sprigs, to garnish

TO SERVE:
lime wedges
tomato, bell pepper, and scallion salad

1 Place the chicken in a nonmetallic dish. To make the marinade, mix the remaining ingredients together in a bowl, seasoning with salt and pepper.

2 Pour the marinade over the chicken, turn to coat well, then leave to marinate for at least an hour at room temperature. If possible leave for 24 hours in the refrigerator to marinate.

3 Remove the chicken from the marinade and pat dry with paper towels.

4 Place the chicken on a pan and place under a preheated broiler for 20-25 minutes, turning once, until the chicken is golden brown on the outside and cooked through. Brush with the marinade occasionally. To test if it is cooked, pierce a thick part with a skewer—the juices should run clear.

5 Garnish with cilantro and serve with lime wedges and a refreshing tomato, bell pepper, and scallion side salad.

Game Hen in Salsa Verde

*Flavored with a green herb marinade, these elegant poussins
are packed with lively Mexican flavors.*

Serves 4

INGREDIENTS

10 garlic cloves, chopped
juice of 1 lime
1 bunch fresh cilantro, finely chopped
½ fresh green chili, deseeded and
   chopped
1 tsp. ground cumin

4 game hens
1½ cups crème fraîche
1 red bell pepper, roasted, peeled,
   deseeded and diced
¼ -1 tsp. marinade from chipotle
   canned in adobo, or chipotle salsa

3-5 scallions, thinly sliced
handful of toasted pumpkin seeds
salt and pepper

1 Combine about 9 garlic cloves with the lime juice, about three quarters of the fresh cilantro, the green chili, and half the cumin in a bowl. Press the mixture on to the game hens and leave to marinate for at least 3 hours in the refrigerator or preferably overnight.

2 Place the game hens in a roasting pan and cook in a preheated oven at 400° F for 15 minutes. Remove one from the oven at this point, to check whether it is cooked: pierce the thigh with a knife and if the juices run clear, the bird is cooked. If necessary, return to the oven and continue to roast until cooked through.

3 Meanwhile, mix the crème fraîche with the bell pepper, chipotle marinade, and remaining garlic and cumin. Set aside.

4 Serve each game hen with a spoonful of the pepper sauce and a sprinkling of the remaining cilantro, the scallions, and pumpkin seeds. Serve right away.

VARIATIONS

For lamb, skewer lamb chunks, such as shoulder or leg, onto metal or soaked bamboo skewers. Marinate in the green herbed marinade as in Step 1, then cook over the hot coals of a grill until the lamb is cooked to your liking. Serve with spicy salsa as desired.

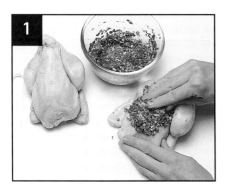

Chicken with Purslane & Red Chili

Purslane is growing in popularity in the West, due to its unique flavor and healthy dose of omega-3 fatty acids. It is a weed, and beloved by the Mexicans, who stew it as well as eat it raw.

Serves 4

INGREDIENTS

juice of 1 lime
6 garlic cloves, finely chopped
¼ tsp. dried oregano
¼ tsp. dried marjoram
¼ tsp. dried thyme
½ tsp. ground cumin
1 chicken, cut into 4 pieces

about 10 large dried mild chilies, such
  as pasilla
2 cups boiling water
2 cups chicken stock
3 tbsp. extra-virgin olive oil
1 lb. 9 oz. tomatoes, charred under
  the broiler, skinned, and deseeded

handful of corn tortilla chips, crushed
several large handfuls of purslane, cut
  into bite-sized lengths
½ lime
salt and pepper
lime wedges, to serve

1 Combine the lime juice, half the garlic, the oregano, marjoram, thyme, cumin, and salt to taste. Rub the mixture over the chicken and leave to marinate for at least an hour, or overnight in the refrigerator.

2 Place the chilies in a pan and pour the boiling water over them. Cover and leave for 30 minutes. Remove the stems and seeds; purée the chilies in a food processor or blender, adding just enough of the stock to make a smooth paste. Add the rest of the stock, mix well, and set aside.

3 Heat a tablespoon of oil in a heavy-based frying pan. Add the chili purée with the tomatoes and remaining garlic. Cook over a medium heat, stirring, until it has reduced by half. Set aside.

4 Remove the chicken from the marinade, reserving any marinade juices. Brown the chicken pieces in the remaining oil, then place in flameproof casserole. Add any reserved marinade juices and the reduced chili sauce. Cover and simmer over a low heat for about 30 minutes until the chicken is tender.

5 Stir the crushed tortillas into the sauce and cook for a few minutes. For smoother texture, process the sauce. Return to the casserole and add the purslane. Season with salt, pepper, and a squeeze of lime.

Duck with Mole Sauce & Pineapple

A wonderful combination of sweet and spicy flavors, this dish is bursting with Mexican flavors.
Serve with a mixture of long-grain and wild rice for a sophisticated touch.

Serves 4

INGREDIENTS

1 duck, cut into 4 pieces
juice of 2 limes
½ cup pineapple juice
5-8 garlic cloves, sliced or chopped

a few shakes of mild red chili powder,
   such as ancho
2 tbsp. sugar
salt

½ pineapple, peeled and cut into slices
2 cups mole sauce (see page 90)
fresh chili strips, to garnish

---

1 Combine the duck with the lime juice, pineapple juice, garlic, chili powder, salt, and half the sugar. Leave to marinate for at least 2 hours, preferably overnight in the refrigerator.

2 Remove the ducks from the marinade and pat dry with paper towels. Arrange the dark meat in a roasting pan and roast in a preheated oven at 325° F for about 20 minutes. Pour off the fat as it renders from the duck.

3 Add the breast pieces and continue to roast slowly for about 20 more minutes. Pour off the fat. Increase the temperature to 400-425° F for 5-10 minutes or long enough to crisp and brown the duck.

4 Warm the mole sauce with enough water to prevent it from sticking and burning. Set aside and keep warm.

5 Sprinkle the pineapple with the remaining sugar and broil

on both sides until the pineapple is lightly browned.

6 Serve the duck portions accompanied by the pineapple slices and topped with the mole sauce. Garnish with chili and serve.

Turkey with Mole

In Mexican groceries you can buy a jar of mole paste—useful for when you don't have a stash of leftover mole in your refrigerator or freezer.

Serves 4

INGREDIENTS

4 turkey pieces or 1 large chicken, cut into 4 pieces
1 onion, chopped
1 whole garlic bulb, cloves divided up and peeled
1 stalk celery, chopped
1 bay leaf

1 bunch cilantro, finely chopped
2¼ cups mole sauce (see page 90) or use ready-made mole, thinned as instructed on the container
about 2 cups chicken stock

TO GARNISH:
4-5 tbsp. sesame seeds
4-5 tbsp. chopped fresh cilantro

1 Arrange the turkey in a large flameproof casserole. Pour the stock and water around the turkey, then add the onion, garlic, celery, bay leaf, and half the cilantro.

2 Cover and bake in a preheated oven at 375° F for about 2 hours; the turkey should be very tender but not dry.

3 Warm the mole in a pan with enough stock to make it the consistency of thin cream.

4 To toast the sesame seeds for the garnish, put the seeds in an ungreased frying pan and fry, shaking the pan, until lightly golden.

5 Arrange the turkey pieces on a serving plate and spoon the warmed mole over the top. Sprinkle with the toasted sesame seeds and chopped fresh cilantro and serve.

Desserts & Beverages

Mexico is a land that swelters in the heat of the sun, and living there one needs constant refreshment and rehydration. The cuisine offers a wealth of drinks to slake this thirst, to refresh, to replenish: drinks based on juices or fruits mixed with milk. For a drink with a bit more punch, try tequila-based Margarita, and on the soothing side, relax with a traditional Mexican hot chocolate.

For dessert, fresh fruit, the amazing fragrant and sweet fresh fruit of Mexico, is often all you'll want, especially after the hearty and satisfying fare of this land. If you yearn for something rich however, try Churros, cinnamon-scented doughnut-like fritters, or little meringues named after the sigh of a nun, Suspiros.

Aztec Oranges

Simplicity itself, this refreshing orange dessert
is hard to beat and is the perfect follow up to a hearty,
spiced main course dish.

Serves 4-6

INGREDIENTS

6 oranges
1 lime
2 tbsp. tequila

2 tbsp. orange-flavored liqueur
dark soft brown sugar, to taste

fine lime rind strips, to decorate
(see Cook's Tip)

1 Using a sharp knife, cut a slice off the top and bottom of the oranges, then remove the peel and pith, cutting downward and taking care to retain the shape of the oranges.

2 Holding the oranges on their side, cut horizontally into slices.

3 Place the oranges in a bowl. Cut the lime in half and squeeze over the oranges. Sprinkle with the tequila and liqueur, then sprinkle over sugar to taste.

4 Chill until ready to serve, then transfer to a serving dish and garnish with lime strips.

COOK'S TIP

To make the decoration, finely pare the rind from a lime using a vegetable peeler, then cut into thin strips. Add to boiling water and blanch for 2 minutes. Drain in a sieve and rinse under cold running water. Drain again and pat dry with paper towels. Use this method for orange and lemon decorative strips as well.

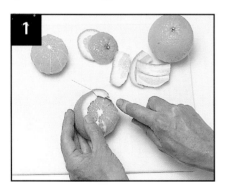

Pineapple Compote with Tequila & Mint

This light, chilled dessert is a refreshing way to finish a Mexican spread.
For a more elaborate dish, accompany the pineapple with a scoop of good-quality pineapple sorbet.

Serves 4–6

INGREDIENTS

1 ripe pineapple
sugar, to taste
juice of 1 lemon

2–3 tbsp. tequila or a few drops of
vanilla extract

several sprigs of fresh mint, leaves
removed and cut into thin strips
fresh mint sprig, to decorate

1 Using a sharp knife, cut off the top and bottom of the pineapple. Place upright on a board, then slice off the skin, cutting downward. Cut in half, remove the core if desired, then cut the flesh into slices. Cut into chunks.

2 Put the pineapple in a bowl and sprinkle with the sugar, lemon juice, tequila, or vanilla extract.

3 Toss the pineapple to coat well, then chill until ready to serve.

4 To serve, arrange on a serving plate and sprinkle with the mint strips. Decorate with a mint sprig.

COOK'S TIP

Make sure you sliced off the "eyes" when removing the skin from the pineapple.

VARIATIONS

Substitute 3 peeled sliced mangoes for the pineapple. To prepare mango, slice of a large piece of flesh on either side of the pit, peel and cut into chunks. Slice off the remaining flesh attached to the pit.

Oranges & Strawberries with Lime

Ideal as a summery dessert, this dish can also be served as a fresh fruit dish with brunch. The oranges enhance the delicate flavor of the berries.

Serves 4

INGREDIENTS

3 sweet oranges
8 oz. strawberries

grated rind and juice of 1 lime
1-2 tbsp. sugar

fresh mint spring, to decorate

1 Using a sharp knife, cut a slice off the top and bottom of the oranges, then remove the peel and pith, cutting downward and taking care to retain the shape of the oranges.

2 Using a small sharp knife, cut down between the membranes of the oranges to remove the segments. Discard the membranes.

3 Hull the strawberries, pulling the leaves off with a pinching action. Cut into slices, along the length of the strawberries.

4 Put the oranges and strawberries in a bowl, then sprinkle with the lime rind, lime juice and sugar. Chill until ready to serve.

5 To serve, transfer to a serving bowl and decorate with a mint sprig.

VARIATIONS

Replace the oranges with mangoes, and the strawberries with blackberries, for a dramatically colored dessert.

COOK'S TIP

An optional hit of orange-flavored liqueur is delicious on this—reduce or omit the sugar.

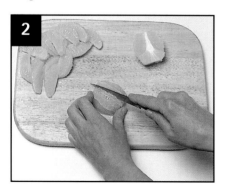

Icy Fruit Blizzard

Keep a store of prepared fruit in the freezer, then whirl it up into this refreshing dessert, which is as light and healthy as it is satisfying. You can vary the fruit as you like.

Serves 4

INGREDIENTS

1 pineapple

1 large piece deseeded watermelon, peeled and cut into small pieces

8 oz. strawberries or other berries, hulled and whole or sliced

1 mango, peach or nectarine, peeled and sliced

1 banana, peeled and sliced

orange juice

sugar, to taste

1 Cover 2 nonstick baking sheets or on ordinary baking sheets with a sheet of plastic wrap. Arrange the fruit on top and freeze for at least 2 hours or until firm and icy.

2 Place one type of fruit in a food processor and process until it is broken up into small pieces.

3 Add a little orange juice and sugar, to taste, and continue to process until it forms a granular mixture. Repeat with the remaining fruit. Arrange in chilled bowls and serve immediately.

COOK'S TIP

The fruit can be processed all together, if preferred, or use just one type of fruit—match the juice to the fruit.

VARIATIONS

For an icy fruit yogurt shake, omit the pineapple and watermelon and process the remaining fruit together, replacing the juice with a half and half mix of milk and fruit yogurt.

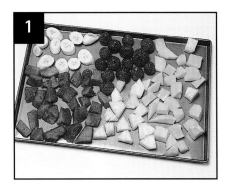

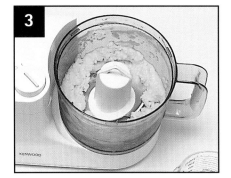

Bunuelo Stars

Cutting the flour tortillas into star shapes makes a whimsical-shaped treat,
and the points of the starts get deliciously crisp.

Serves 4

INGREDIENTS

4 flour tortillas
3 tbsp. ground cinnamon

6-8 tbsp. sugar
vegetable oil, for frying

chocolate ice cream, to serve
fine orange rind strips, to decorate

1 Using a sharp knife or kitchen scissors cut each tortilla into star shapes.

2 Mix the cinnamon and sugar together and set aside.

3 Heat the oil in a shallow, wide frying pan until it is hot enough to brown a cube of bread in 30 seconds. Working one at a time, fry the star-shaped tortillas until one side is golden, then turn and cook until golden on the other side. Remove from the hot oil with a slotted spoon and drain on paper towels.

4 Sprinkle generously with the cinnamon and sugar mixture. Serve chocolate ice cream, sprinkled with orange rind strips.

COOK'S TIP

These star-shaped bunuelos make an attractive decoration for an ice cream sundae with Mexican flavors, caramel, cinnamon, coffee, chocolate.

VARIATIONS

Drench the bunuelos in a simple syrup, flavored with a little cinnamon or aniseed.

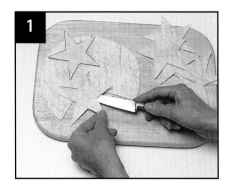

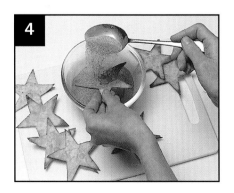

Empanadas of Banana & Chocolate

Using phyllo pastry makes these empanadas light and crisp on the outside, while the filling of diced banana and bits of chocolate melts into a scrumptious hot banana-chocolate goo.

Serves 4-6

INGREDIENTS

about 8 sheets of phyllo pastry, cut into half lengthways
melted butter or vegetable oil, for brushing

2 ripe sweet bananas
1-2 tsp. sugar
juice of ¼ lemon
6-7 oz. plain chocolate, broken into

small pieces
powdered sugar, for dusting
ground cinnamon, for dusting

1 Working one at a time, lay a long rectangular sheet of phyllo out in front of you and brush it with butter or oil.

2 Peel and dice and bananas and place in a bowl. Add the sugar and lemon juice and stir well to combine. Stir in the chocolate.

3 Place a couple of teaspoons of the banana and chocolate mixture in one corner of the pastry, then fold over into a triangle shape to enclose the filling. Continue to fold in a triangular shape, until the phyllo is completely wrapped around the filling.

4 Dust with powdered sugar and cinnamon. Place on a baking sheet and continue the process with the remaining phyllo and filling.

5 Bake in a preheated oven at 375° F for about 15 minutes or until the little pastries are golden. Remove from the oven and serve hot—warn people that the filling is very hot.

COOK'S TIP

You could use ready-made puff pastry instead of phyllo for a more fluffy effect.

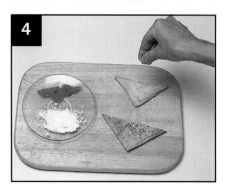

Churros

Sold on the streets of Mexico, these tempting treats can be enjoyed at any time of the day—dip them into a cup of hot chocolate for breakfast, nibble them as a mid-day snack with coffee, or serve them as part of a late-night supper.

Serves 4

INGREDIENTS

1 cup water
rind of 1 lemon
6 tbsp. butter
⅛ tsp. salt

1 cup all-purpose flour
¼ tsp. ground cinnamon, plus extra
   for dusting
½-1 tsp. vanilla extract

3 eggs
olive oil, for frying
about 5 tbsp. sugar

1 Place the water with the lemon rind in a heavy-based saucepan. Bring to a boil, add the butter and salt and cook for a few moments until the butter melts.

2 Add the flour all at once, with the cinnamon and vanilla, then remove the pan from the heat and stir rapidly until it forms the consistency of mashed potatoes.

3 Beat in the eggs, one at a time, using a wooden spoon; if you have difficulty incorporating the eggs to a smooth mixture, use a potato masher, then when it is mixed, return to a wooden spoon and mix until smooth.

4 Heat 1 inch oil in a deep frying pan until it is hot enough to brown a cube of bread in 30 seconds.

5 Place the batter in a pastry tube with a wide nozzle, then squeeze out 5 inch lengths directly into the hot oil, making sure that the churros are about 3-4 inches apart, as they will puff up as they cook. You may need fry them in 2 or 3 batches.

6 Cook the churros in the hot oil for about 2 minutes on each side, until they are golden brown. Remove with a slotted spoon and drain on paper towels.

7 Dust generously with sugar and sprinkle with cinnamon to taste. Serve either hot or at room temperature.

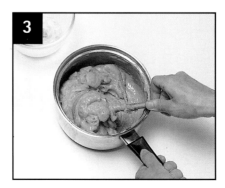

Torta de Cielo

This flat almond-flavored sponge cake has a dense, moist texture which melts in the mouth. The perfect accompaniment to a good strong cup of coffee for either brunch or afternoon tea.

Serves 4–6

INGREDIENTS

6 oz. raw almonds, in their skins
2 sticks unsalted butter, at room temperature
1 cup plus 2 tbsp. sugar
3 eggs, lightly beaten
1 tsp. almond extract

1 tsp. vanilla extract
9 tbsp. all-purpose flour
a pinch of salt
butter, for greasing

TO SERVE:
powdered sugar, for dusting
slivered almonds, toasted

1 Lightly butter an 8 inch round or square cake pan and line with baking parchment.

2 Put the almonds in a food processor to form a "crumbly" mixture. Set aside.

3 Beat together the butter and sugar in a bowl until smooth and fluffy. Beat in the eggs, almonds, and almond and vanilla extracts until well blended.

4 Stir in the flour and salt and mix briefly, until the flour is just incorporated.

5 Pour or spoon the batter into the greased pan and smooth the surface. Bake in a preheated oven at 350° F for 40-50 minutes or until the cake feels spongy when gently pressed.

6 Remove from the oven, and leave to cool on a wire rack to cool. To serve, dust with powdered sugar and decorate with toasted almonds.

Mexican Chocolate Meringues

*The Mexican name for these delicate meringues is suspiros, meaning "sighs"—
allegedly the contented sighs of the nuns who created them.
They are lightly crisp on the outside, with a deliciously chewy texture centre.*

Makes about 25 meringues

INGREDIENTS

4-5 egg whites, at room temperature
a pinch of salt
¼ tsp. cream of tartar
¼-½ tsp. vanilla extract

6-7 oz. superfine sugar
⅛-¼ tsp. ground cinnamon
4 oz. plain or semi-sweet chocolate,
  grated

TO SERVE:
ground cinnamon
4 oz. strawberries
chocolate-flavored cream
(see Cook's Tip)

1 Whisk the egg whites until they are foamy, then add the salt and cream of tartar and beat until very stiff. Whisk in the vanilla, then slowly whisk in the sugar, a small amount at a time, until the meringue is shiny and stiff. This should take about 3 minutes by hand, and under a minute with an electric beater.

2 Whisk in the cinnamon and grated chocolate. Spoon mounds, about 2 tablespoonfuls, on to an ungreased nonstick baking sheet. Space the mounds well.

3 Place in a preheated oven at 300° F and cook for 3 hours until set.

4 Carefully remove from the baking sheet. If the meringues are too moist and soft, return them to the oven to firm up and dry out more. Allow to cool completely.

5 Serve the meringues dusted with cinnamon and accompanied by strawberries and chocolate-flavored cream.

COOK'S TIP

To make the flavored cream, simply stir half-melted chocolate pieces into stiffly whipped cream, then chill until solid.

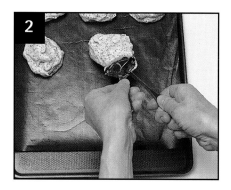

Mexican Milk Drinks

Two milky drinks, packed with authentic Mexican flavors—
choose a cooling strawberry milkshake for a hot summer's day,
or a rich hot chocolate drink, with spicy aromas, as a winter warmer.

Serves 4

INGREDIENTS

STRAWBERRY MILKSHAKE:

1 lb. strawberries

3 cups milk

1 cup strawberry yogurt (optional)

sugar, to taste

2 handfuls of ice cubes

MEXICAN HOT CHOCOLATE:

4-6 oz. plain chocolate, broken into
  small pieces

½ tsp. ground cinnamon

4 cups milk

dash of almond extract

dash of vanilla extract

just a few grains of salt (to bring out
  the flavor of the chocolate)

sugar, to taste

2 tbsp. grated chocolate

4 cinnamon sticks, to serve (optional)

1 To make the strawberry milkshake, place the strawberries in a blender or food processor, reserving 4 for decoration. Add the milk and yogurt, if using, to the blender and process to a purée.

2 Add sugar, to taste, and the ice cubes, then blend again until the ice is crushed and the drink is thick and icy. Pour into tall glasses, decorate with the reserved strawberries and serve at once.

3 To make the Mexican chocolate, gently heat the chocolate with the cinnamon and milk in a saucepan.

4 When the chocolate has melted, add the almond and vanilla extracts with the salt and sugar. Whisk together until well blended and heated through.

5 Pour into cups, sprinkle with grated chocolate, and serve each cup with a cinnamon stick for stirring, if wished.

VARIATIONS

To vary the flavor of the milkshake, substitute raspberries, bananas or mango, for the strawberries and use a yogurt of your choice.

Fruit Refreshers

A creamy coconut milk drink and classic Sangria are given a Mexican twist with the addition of fragrant lime and exotic tropical fruit.

Serves 4-6

INGREDIENTS

COCONUT-LIME DRINK:
2 cups coconut milk (unsweetened)
1 cup freshly squeezed lime juice
4 cups tropical fruit juice, such as mango, papaya, guava, or passion fruit
sugar, to taste
crushed ice
fresh mint sprigs, to decorate

SANGRIA:
1 bottle dry full-bodied red wine
¼ cup orange-flavored liqueur and brandy
¼ cup brandy
1 cup orange juice
sugar, to taste
1 orange, washed
1 lime, washed

1 peach or nectarine
1 mango
½ cucumber, thinly sliced
ice cubes
bubbly mineral water, for topping up

1 To make the coconut-lime fruit drink, combine the coconut milk with the lime juice, tropical fruit juice, and sugar, to taste. Add the ice and whisk until well mixed. Alternatively, place the ingredients in a food processor and process until well mixed. Serve immediately, decorated with mint leaves.

2 To make the sangria, pour the wine into a punch bowl and mix in the liqueur, brandy, orange juice, and sugar, to taste. Cover and chill to infuse for a few hours.

3 Slice the orange and lime widthways. Cut the peach in half, remove the stone and slice the flesh. Peel the mango, then slice the flesh from the pit.

4 Add the prepared fruit, cucumber, and ice cubes to the punch bowl and top up with mineral water. Serve at once.

COOK'S TIP

Turn the coconut-lime drink into an alcoholic cocktail: add 2 tablespoons white rum per person. Add an extra decoration of tropical fruit pieces, threaded on to bamboo skewers.

Classic Margaritas

Margaritas are what makes a hot and sultry Mexican afternoon not only tolerable, but something to look forward to. A tropical holiday in a glass.

Serves 2

INGREDIENTS

CLASSIC MARGARITAS:
pared lime or lemon peel
salt, for dipping
1½ tbsp. tequila
1½ tbsp. orange-flavored liqueur
3 tbsp. freshly squeezed lime juice
handful of cracked ice
fine strips of lime rind, to decorate

MELON MARGARITAS:
1 small flavorful cantaloupe melon
   peeled, deseeded, and diced
several large handfuls of ice
juice of 1 lime
scant ½ cup tequila
sugar, to taste

FROZEN PEACH MARGARITAS:
1 peach, sliced and frozen, or an equal
   amount of purchased frozen
   peaches
2 tbsp. tequila
¼ cup peach or orange-flavored
   liqueur
juice of ½ lime
diced fresh peach or 1-2 tbsp. orange
   juice, if needed

1 To make the classic margaritas, moisten the rim of two shallow, stemmed glasses with the lime or lemon peel, then dip the edge of the glasses in salt. Shake off the excess.

2 Put the tequila in a blender or food processor with the liqueur, lime juice, and cracked ice. Process to blend well.

3 Pour the drink into the prepared glasses, taking care not to disturb the salt-coated rim. If preferred, strain the drink before pouring into the glass. Decorate with lime rind and serve.

4 To make the melon margaritas. Put the melon in a food processor and process to form a purée. Add the ice, lime juice,

tequila, and sugar to taste and process until smooth. Pour the drink into chilled shallow glasses.

5 To make the frozen peach margaritas, blend the frozen fruit, tequila, liqueur, and lime juice in a food processor until a thick purée. If too thick, add diced peach or orange juice to thin. Pour into chilled glasses and serve.

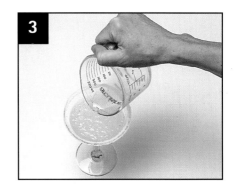

Index